THOUGHT FIELD THERAPY

Clinical Applications

Integrating TFT in Psychotherapy Practice

Suzanne M. Connolly, LCSW, LMFT

George Tyrrell Press

For further information, contact the author at:
Suzanne M. Connolly
70 Payne Place, Suite 6
Sedona, AZ 86336
928-282-2627
zanne@sedona.net

Suzanne M. Connolly, LCSW, LMFT
Thought Field Therapy

1. Author 2. Title 3. Real Estate
Library of Congress Control Number: 2004106833
ISBN: 0-9755591-0-9

The cases discussed in this book are based on actual cases. The names and other possible identifying information such as occupations and ages have been changed to protect client confidentiality. Any resemblances to actual persons are entirely coincidental.

Acknowledgements

This book began long ago, when, as a thirty-some-year-old mother of six children, I stepped through the doors of Northern Arizona University. To be specific, I stepped through the front doors of the psychology building. I stopped, took a mental snapshot and thought: *I will remember this moment for the rest of my life*. All journeys begin with a single step and that was the beginning of this particular journey. I would like to thank those who have helped me along the way.

I want to express gratitude to my husband of 43 years, Bruce John Connolly. Bruce not only put up with me for all those years but it was thanks to his encouragement that I took the leap and learned to do this "strange new technique."

Thanks to former workshop assistant, Merry Barr, fellow TFT trainer, Jill Strunk who perused the manuscript and made many helpful suggestions, and Sophia Tarila who proofed and edited.

Thanks also to my European friend Gloria Monda who first encouraged me to write the book and who gave me a bedroom and office space in Rotterdam to work on this manuscript without interruption.

And last, but not least, I want to express my deepest appreciation to the many clients, past and present, who have blessed me with their presence and taught me more than they will ever know.

This book is dedicated to those who use their talents in the service of others; those who use their gift of healing to ease the psychological burdens of others; those who are great at what they do but are never satisfied in their quest to make the healing process an ever more positive one. May this book help you in your desire to make a difference.

I would also like to dedicate this book to Dr. Roger J. Callahan. This book would not have been possible had it not been for the work of Dr. Callahan, who gifted the world with a truly new approach to psychotherapy. I am grateful for the privilege of knowing him.

It is very seldom that something so new and different is discovered. Thought Field Therapy is beginning to move the therapy world. It is something akin to a subtle pressure building beneath the surface of that world. I predict that there will be an earthquake before long and that, when the aftershocks cease, we will find the landscape of the therapy world forever changed.

Suzanne M. Connolly

THOUGHT FIELD THERAPY

Clinical Applications

Integrating TFT in Psychotherapy Practice

Contents

FOREWORD

Suzanne Connolly is a highly experienced psychotherapist. She has been associated with Thought Field Therapy® (TFT) for nearly a decade, attending one of our first diagnostic level trainings in 1995. Suzanne has been teaching approved TFT algorithm level trainings longer than any other trainer. I have often received very positive feedback from those who have attended her courses.

A brief background: In the clinical psychology training program at SyracuseUniversity in the early 1950's, I was trained in Carl Rogers Client-Centered Therapy. I later searched for a more active and effective therapy and I met Albert Ellis. I became one of the first to promote this work and I helped Al Ellis train others in the early days. Ellis was the first therapist to do what is now called Cognitive Therapy. Though pleased with Ellis' approach, I was still not fully satisfied. I kept looking and finally began developing my own brand of treatment in 1979. Though I was looking for something better, in my wildest dreams as a psychotherapist, I never thought that there could be a psychological treatment that would instantly eliminate all traces of severe and chronic psychological problems. At first it was difficult for me to believe the reality of my results; but repeated observations forced me. It should be obvious that the treatment success of Thought Field Therapy®has vast implications for theoretical understanding. For example, the immediacy of the treatments, faster than chemical reactions could be, raises serious questions about the common chemical theories. Although chemistry is basic and important, it is not the deepest or fundamental level. TFT has introduced a number of new and startling facts into psychology. Suzanne Connolly is highly skilled and has had excellent results using TFT in her psychotherapy practice for nine years. I am pleased she became interested in my work for she is a highly competent professional, both in her practice and her teaching.

I have seen her teaching and skills improve over the years. She not only has returned to attend numerous Diagnostic Level and Advanced Level TFT trainings to improve her education and skills, she did something very interesting. Suzanne brought me a video tape of her teaching the course. She asked me to go over it and make comments. I believe she always strives for excellence in her teachings and understanding of TFT. Her book is full of practical advice and contains many tips on applying TFT algorithms effectively to help various psychological problems. Any one interested in applying my TFT algorithms to help various problems is well-advised to obtain this book. Suzanne has done a marvelous job.

Roger Callahan
Indian Wells, CA, 2004

INTRODUCTION

Pouring New Wine into Old Wineskins

There is a passage in the Christian New Testament that warns of pouring new wine into old wineskins. It is the ruin of both the new wine and the old wineskin. The old wineskin breaks and the new wine is spilled. There is nothing to be gained and everything to be lost. Radically new ideas can be like that. The old must often be dispensed with, because the old is limiting and cannot expand to embrace the new. The new is difficult to accept. We love our old ways of looking at the world, our old ways of doing things, our old behaviors. They are dear to us and bring us the comfort and security that comes with knowing that we have constructed a view of the world, a method of doing things, a pattern of behavior that has brought a certain order and meaning to our own personal universe.

As a species, it took us some time to get used to the idea that the sun didn't revolve around the earth as the Egyptians and other ancient cultures had believed for thousands of years. More recently, even Einstein had difficulty believing that at the sub-atomic level there was a certain amount of unpredictability in the universe, as Chaos Theory hypothesized. Today there are very few members of The

Flat Earth Society and few in science who question the unpredictability of events at the quantum level.

In the world of psychotherapy a radical new discovery was made in 1979. Roger J. Callahan discovered that tapping on the end of a client's energy meridian, her stomach meridian, to be precise, cured her of a debilitating, lifelong fear of water. More than 20 years later we have, as the result of that discovery, the precise science of Thought Field Therapy, which involves tapping specific energy meridians in a specific sequence to alleviate psychological problems. This method of treating problems is predictably difficult to accept. It flies in the face of many deeply ingrained beliefs. For instance, we believe that "there is no such thing as a quick fix." We believe that we "have to suffer to get better" and "if something sounds too good to be true, well, it probably is. "

The more experience we have had in life, the more dearly we hold these beliefs, because life in general reinforces them. But, while it is usually true that "if something sounds too good to be true, it probably is," we must remain open to life's surprises.

I can remember answering a phone call one day when I was in my early 20s. The male voice on the other end was telling me I had won an all-expense-paid trip for two to San Francisco. I couldn't remember entering any such contest and almost hung up on him. Luckily for my husband and me, I didn't. A few weeks later we were staying at the Mark Hopkins Hotel in San Francisco, driving a red Mustang, and enjoying our free, much needed, no-strings-attached vacation in our favorite city. Sometimes things that sound too good to be true really are true. Such is the case with Thought Field Therapy.

The “we have to suffer to get better” belief seems specifically dear to the mental health field. Physicians devote their lives to the goal of easing the suffering of their patients and have no problem prescribing the “quick fix” of antibiotics, pain medication, or some other medication designed to spare physical or mental suffering. Indeed, physicians are sometimes accused of being too ready to dispense some of the “quick fix” medications mentioned above. In the field of mental health this belief may reflect only our previous limitations in working with clients who are deeply wounded and whom we previously treated with the only tools we had, not the least of which consisted of our love, our compassion, our insight, and our support.

Despite logic, we cling to the old (although it is also true that despite logic some cling to the new, just because it is new). It is no surprise that rational, thinking people have some difficulty embracing this new method of doing psychotherapy. If you are reading this book it is likely that you have already embraced the notion of using Thought Field Therapy, because you have experienced firsthand the results of using these techniques.

There is no attempt made in the following pages to convince those who are skeptical of Thought Field Therapy (TFT) that this is an effective, efficient, helpful or otherwise worthwhile psychotherapy technique. A discussion of current research in regards to Thought Field Therapy is beyond the scope of this book. It is, perhaps, the topic for an entirely different manuscript to be written in the future. For a brief summary of research involving Thought Field Therapy, please refer to Appendix IV.

The following pages have been written for the professional mental health or medical practitioner who is trained at the minimum at the algorithm level of Thought Field Therapy, or has read Dr. Roger Callahan's book, *Tapping the Healer Within*. This book has been written with the intention of enhancing the already trained reader's skills in using Thought Field Therapy in a clinical setting.

While the paradigm of using Thought Field Therapy to treat mental distress in no way fits into previous paradigms of psychotherapy (there simply is no fit), we can pour this new wine into old wineskins while keeping the integrity of both, without splitting the old wine-skin and without spilling the precious new wine.

This book is designed to be a how-to manual on just that.

CHAPTER 1

Mixing the Old With the New

"The benevolence of Natural Law lies in assuring us that.miracles are open to us, but it does not extend to telling us how to accomplish them; it is for us to discover the keys, the encodings and the decodings, by which they are brought to pass."

Robert Rosen, Theoretical biologist, *Life Itself: A Comprehensive Inquiry in the Nature, Origin and Fabrication of Life*

❖ ❖ ❖ ❖

Brief therapy techniques such as Thought Field Therapy should never be thought of as substitutes for good personal therapy skills. When I give workshops, I emphasize that the most important tool a therapist brings into therapy is his or herself. This human connection is a cornerstone of both the old and the new. However, Thought Field

Therapy can dramatically enhance a good therapist's ability to treat clients successfully. At times Thought Field Therapy can simply shorten the length of treatment and make good therapy even better. At other times, Thought Field Therapy can produce results nothing short of miraculous.

Many therapists have been trained in Thought Field Therapy but they are not yet sure how these new techniques can fit into more traditional ways of delivering mental health services. Many therapists report to me, for instance, that they are confused as to how Thought Field Therapy can enhance couple therapy, sex therapy or help individuals overcome issues involving low self-esteem.

Other questions frequently asked are: "When several issues are presented, how do I decide which issue to work on first?", "What do I do if another problem comes up before we are finished working on the original problem?", "Can we work on more than one emotion at a time?", and "How do I combine the various algorithms?" In the section called *FAQ,* I will attempt to answer some of these frequently asked questions. And hopefully you will find as you read the case studies included in the chapters of this book that you are getting a feel about how to integrate Thought Field Therapy into the good work that you are already doing.

At this time in my career as a therapist I lean heavily on Thought Field Therapy as my brief therapy treatment of choice. Although I am trained in many other brief therapy techniques such as EMDR (Eye Movement Desensitization and Reprocessing), TIR, (Trauma Incident Reduction), and NLP (Neuro Linguistic Programming), I find that Thought Field Therapy is fast, effective, fits well into a therapy hour, doesn't need a lot of preparation and is easy to introduce to the client. It usually involves very little distress to the client or therapist compared to other therapies such as Systematic Desensitization, Exposure Therapy or EMDR.

I use Thought Field Therapy with almost every client that I see and I usually use Thought Field Therapy to treat several different issues with an individual client. However, I integrate Thought Field Therapy into my more traditional approach to individual therapy, sex therapy and couple therapy. And I sometimes combine Thought Field Therapy with a sprinkling of the other brief therapy techniques, such as Neuro-Linguistic Programming and Ericksonian Hypnotherapy techniques.

In addition to using Thought Field Therapy to treat clients in my private practice, I've had the good fortune to have given over 100 professional trainings in Thought Field Therapy. During these trainings, professionals work on their own individual issues, so it is safe to say that I have used Thought Field Therapy thousands of times. During the trainings and in my practice, I witness very few instances where Thought Field Therapy does not accomplish the stated goal of the client pertaining to working on a specific problem.

While I do not get follow up with all clients, I get enough positive feedback from clients and previous clients about the lasting results of Thought Field Therapy that I feel confident using it, and I would feel negligent not offering this powerful therapeutic tool to my clients.

The trainings that I offer to professionals at this time involve teaching therapists at the algorithm level, the most basic level of Thought Field Therapy. In almost all cases, as professionals work on their own problems and each other's problems during the trainings, the algorithms alone are effective. Because I have been trained by Dr. Roger Callahan at the diagnostic level of Thought Field Therapy, I have the added advantage of using this more advanced level of Thought Field Therapy (TFTdx) in my private practice, in those cases when the simple algorithms do not work.The (diagnostic level of Thought Field Therapy is the level in which a unique and advanced form of muscle testing developed by Dr. Roger J. Callahan is used to determine where a client needs to tap their body and in what order.) Therapists reading this book who are trained at the diagnostic level of Thought Field Therapy can also benefit from the case studies presented in the following chapters. Therapists trained at this more advanced level may choose, when appropriate, to treat similar cases using TFTdx rather than the simple, but slightly less effective algorithms.

In my workshops as well as in my private practice, I occasionally refer to therapists who are trained in and have the equipment necessary to do Thought Field Therapy Voice Technology (VT) when even the highly specific diagnostic procedures have not been effective. This level of treatment is reserved for the most difficult to treat clients (those who do not respond to either the algorithm procedure or the diagnostic procedure). In most cases these situations are complicated by physical problems, such as Fibromyalgia, Chronic Fatigue or severe allergies.

Chapter 2

Talk Therapy and Thought Field Therapy

"To respect a person is not possible without knowing him: care and responsibility would be blind if they were not guided by knowledge."

Erich Fromm, *The Art of Loving*

❖ ❖ ❖ ❖

This chapter will give you an example of how to set up a problem using talk therapy so that Thought Field Therapy can be used to address a psychological problem effectively and efficiently. This chapter will also give you an idea of how to introduce Thought Field Therapy to your client.

To get the best results using Thought Field Therapy, and this is especially true if you are trained only in using algorithms, it is helpful to be aware that there are three phases of therapy involved. The stages are described as follows:

1. **Determining what the problem is.**

   Occasionally a client will enter therapy with a precise and well thought out goal in mind. However, more frequently part of our job as therapy professionals is to help the client identify exactly what it is they want to change and what a successful outcome would look like. Some helpful questions can be: "What would you like to be different in your life?", "Given the fact that you can't change that other person (only they can change themselves), how would you like to feel given they do what they do/ are who they are/ say what they say/ have the limitations they have?" And, for family therapy: "If I had a magic wand (which I don't) and you were able to change one thing about your family, what would it be?"

   Once goals are defined, it can be helpful to ask the client what they think is getting in the way of them achieving their goal(s). "What do you think gets in the way of your organizing your desk?", "Filing your reports?", "Cleaning your room?", "Getting a job?"

   As you have probably experienced, you usually need to do some talk therapy to get there. Traditional talk therapy can help us to more efficiently prepare to use Thought Field Therapy.

2. **Using the Thought Field Therapy itself.**

   This is the easy part; however, when problems have layers and they frequently do, you will find yourself alternating between the first phase, setting up the problem, and the second phase, doing the Thought Field Therapy tapping sequences themselves.

3. **Follow up.**

   This can include taking a SUD (subjective units of distress) level after an apparently successful treatment and challenging this change by asking a client to try to work up some upset or anxiousness or anger about whatever they were thinking about while doing the Thought Field Therapy. Sometime when a client begins to scan the issue they were working on, new layers come up such as anger or sadness, which the client may not have even been aware of previously. And so the therapist may find that he or she is alternating between the second phase and the third phase or even repeating all three stages with a slightly different or very different problem. Most importantly, it includes testing the results over time and to exposure.

Following is a case story that illustrates the importance of setting up the problem before beginning the Thought Field Therapy intervention.

Using the Three Stages of Thought Field Therapy with a Child Who Is Failing in School

Jake was eleven years old and in serious danger of failing fifth grade. The young man had already been held back one year and his parents were frantic. His mother, Anita, was convinced that Jake's academic failure was a direct result of his anger because she and Jake's father hadn't been getting along. Anita felt that this hypothetical anger had been getting in the way of Jake focusing during school and caring about his homework. It was a good guess and I speculated that passive aggressive behavior could indeed be at play.

Jake's father Juan, an industrious entrepreneur, attributed Jake's behavior to laziness. He was coming down hard on his son and Anita felt scared and in the middle. Anita didn't like Juan's approach and it wasn't working, but nothing she had tried had been effective either.

Anita had come in by herself to explain this situation and to ask if I thought TFT might help her son. Anita had achieved great results using TFT the previous year in overcoming various problems including hurt and anxiety about ways members of her extended family treated her, a driving phobia, and getting angry with her husband and children. I explained to Anita that while I couldn't guarantee that I could help Jake with his school problems, I would be optimistic that by using TFT I could.

When Jake came in for his first session he was quiet and subdued. He would politely answer questions but he did not volunteer any information, especially about his problems at school. Using a "question and answer technique" I learned that he was as confused as everyone else as to why he wasn't doing well in school. Jake finally volunteered that he suspected that he just wasn't as smart as the other children in his class. "When I turn things in it's always full of mistakes." "What kind of mistakes?" I asked. He listed spelling and especially punctuation and sentence structure as problems. "No matter how hard I try, I just can't get it," Jake said.

However, Jake was a good reader and although Hispanic, he was second and third generation, so English as a second language was not an issue. While acknowledging that his parents' difficulties did cause him some sadness and anxiety, he denied being angry. This young man seemed like he really did want to do well in school and it seemed that something besides anger or "laziness" was at work here.

As we limped along using our questioning and answering method I learned that Jake often did his homework and frequently even took his finished homework to school. But fearing (apparently correctly so) that his homework would be unacceptable (full of mistakes in punctuation and spelling), he did not turn in his homework. I began to suspect that there was an anxiety here that was circular. A kind of conditioned response had occurred. Jake now had anxiety around school itself. The anxiety kept him from learning and performing well. And of course this anxiety kept him from turning in the homework. Which, of course, caused more anxiety so the problem was self-perpetuating.

I asked Jake to think about handing in a paper at school. (At least he would, I reasoned, get credit for turning his homework in and perhaps he would get some extra help. And hopefully, if there was no anxiety present, he could learn from any mistakes he made on his papers.) He could not get in touch with any anxiety. I asked him to think about writing an assignment (Jake had a book report that was due at the end of the week). Still-no anxiety. I asked Jake to tell me about the book that he had read. He did a magnificent job of describing the story in great detail. I grabbed a piece of paper and a pen and asked Jake to write down what he had just said. Jake froze. The look on his face was one of terror. We had just completed phase one of setting up a problem and we were now ready to use phase two, actually using Thought Field Therapy to address the problem.

We used that trauma/anxiety algorithm and Jake's SUD level of nine was reduced to a one. That is until I, once again, brought out the paper and pen and asked Jake to write his report. Jake reported a SUD level of four as he looked at the paper and held the pen in his hand. We did a mini reversal and, again, used the trauma/anxiety algorithm. Jake was now anxiety free and ready to write his report. Jake wrote a small part of his book report in the office. The spelling was fine, the punctuation correct. We were now ready for phase three: testing out the problem in a real life situation and seeing if our anxiety cure lasted over time.

The next time we met Jake brought in his finished book report as I had requested. He had handed it in on time and received an A. Writing the assignment had seemed easy for him and he reported that somehow he had "just remembered" how to spell and punctuate.

I met with Jake a third time and then we agreed to meet only if his writing phobia returned. Almost two years later Anita made an appointment to see me to work on a new problem. She nonchalantly mentioned that Jake was doing well. He had passed fifth grade and had been doing very well in school since our sessions.

The preceding case study illustrates how important it can be to set up the problem to be worked on as succinctly and as accurately as possible. If we had worked on Jake's hypothetical anger we would not have achieved these same results. If we had worked on his "laziness" Jake would have been in therapy a long time. Being a good detective is part of doing good therapy even when you have the most sophisticated of therapy interventions at your fingertips.

Jake's Thought Field Therapy Recipe

Trauma/Anxiety
Eyebrow, eye, arm, collarbone
9-Gamut Treatment
Eyebrow, eye, arm, collarbone

Using The Three Phases of TFT in Couple Therapy

A second case study also demonstrates the importance of correctly identifying a problem before attempting the Thought Field Therapy intervention. In this second case a man had called and asked if I would see him and his wife in couple therapy. He explained that he was recently retired, his wife was unhappy and he knew he had to do something different if his marriage was to be saved.

During their first session Meg sobbed as she listed the things that were "wrong" with her husband Ralph. Meg reported that Ralph was controlling and that he frequently spoke to her in a demeaning manner. There was a constant state of tension in the home. It was becoming more than Meg felt she could bear. When I enquired about typical situations when this occurred, a common theme began to emerge. Ralph's tirades took place when they would be getting ready to go somewhere or do something. As they were active socially these incidents were of course common. Ralph was painfully impatient. With a little more questioning I learned that Ralph could never be late for anything; in fact Ralph had to be early wherever he went. When he and Meg attended a party or dinner engagement Ralph would insist that they arrive even earlier than the invited time. Ralph made sure that he and Meg left much earlier than needed to go to the airport or on a road-trip.

For Meg this was a problem because Ralph would be irritated with her if she weren't ready when Ralph thought she should be ready. He would begin getting irritated way before their departure time. Ralph's irritability resulted in tension between Ralph and Meg. Meg would feel belittled and put down by Ralph's controlling behavior. Meg felt like she was losing her sense of self. Both Ralph and Meg felt that their marriage was in crisis.

It was a relief to both Meg and Ralph that I could say to them that their marriage was not in crisis and it didn't need fixing. Their marriage was doing just what relationships are supposed to do. It was working quite well. Relationships offer us opportunities to grow. There was an opportunity for each of them here. Ralph had a simple phobia, I offered, and hopefully this would be easy to fix using Thought Field Therapy. And, of course Meg needed to learn to handle her own anxiety when Ralph wasn't behaving the way she felt he should behave.

This resonated with Ralph who volunteered that during his formative years his father had impressed upon him that it was a terrible thing to waste his or other peoples' time. With a little help, Meg was able to understand that she couldn't control Ralph's behavior but she could control her anxiety and stay centered even if Ralph was reacting. In this way she would not feel in danger of "losing herself."

With phase one completed we were ready to dive right in during our second session and use Thought Field Therapy to address Ralph's phobia: his anxiety about being late. Ralph responded well to the simple anxiety/anger algorithm and later, Meg to the past trauma/anxiety algorithm.

Their complex problems had been reduced to quite simple ones and the TFT intervention went quite well. With phase two completed, at least as far as we could tell we were ready for phase three, actually testing out the problem in real life situations over time. However, as the couple would be traveling we did not make a follow up appointment.

Six months later, Meg called to make an appointment of an entirely different nature. She described how much happier they were and shared that many of their friends had commented on how much more relaxed Ralph was. One friend had commented: "He's like a different person." Phase three had been successfully completed.

This case study demonstrates the value of finding the common denominator when a series of complaints are presented. And this case study clearly illustrates the three stages necessary to use Thought Field Therapy effectively and efficiently.

Ralph's Thought Field Therapy Recipe

Anxiety/Anger
Eye, arm, collarbone, little finger, collarbone
9-Gamut Treatment
Eye, arm, collarbone, little finger, collarbone

Meg's Thought Field Therapy Recipe

Past Trauma/Anxiety:
Eyebrow, eye, arm, collarbone
9-Gamut Treatment
Eyebrow, eye, arm, collarbone

Introducing The TFT Procedure to Clients

Many therapists are initially intimidated about actually introducing Thought Field Therapy to their clients. I get asked about this in almost every presentation that I give.

The following is a typical and deliberately overly simple example of using talk therapy during the first phase in preparation for using Thought Field Therapy: Unlike all other case studies in this book, the following is not an actual case study but rather contains many commonly occurring elements from typical cases familiar to every therapist. We'll assume the client has never heard of Thought Field Therapy and needs to be introduced to TFT during the course of the session.

A client may present saying:

Client: "I have a lot of anger. I want to work on not being so angry all the time."

Therapist: "Who are you angry with? or "What are you angry about?"

Client: "I'm angry at everybody."

Therapist: "What bothers you most about everybody?"

Client: "People always let you down. They never do what they say they are going to do."

Therapist: "Sounds like you get really disappointed when people don't do exactly what they say they are going to do."

Client: "Yeah!"

Therapist: "What was it like growing up? Did your parents usually do what they said they would do?"

Client; “Well, I didn’t have a father living at home. My parents never married and my father eventually married someone much younger and had his own family. He didn’t have anything to do with me when I was growing up. I looked him up and we talk now and then, but I usually initiate the call and he’s pretty busy with his own family.”

Therapist: “How do you feel about that? Do you have any anger toward him? Or do you feel any sadness about this?”

Client: “Not really. I think I’m mostly angry at my mother.”

Therapist: “Tell me more.”

Client: “She was always working and was never there for me. When she was home she was drinking and I didn’t want to be around her. I tried to stay out of her way because she was always getting upset with me. She would promise me something, like a new pair of shoes, but she would blow the money on alcohol instead. She would tell me we would go somewhere, but she would start drinking and forget that she had promised me that we could go. I was embarrassed to bring friends home so I didn’t have many friends.”

Therapist: “Are you angry about this?”

Client: “Yeah. I’m still angry even though she’s no longer alive. In fact I’m angry that she drank herself to death and missed out on being here to see her grandchildren.”

Therapist: “Sounds like things were really difficult growing up and you wish, of course, that it could have been different and that it could be different now. I'm sorry that it wasn't different for you growing up and that you had so little nurturing during your childhood. It must have been very hard to cope with at the time."

Client: "Yes. But I guess others have had it harder."

Therapist: "That doesn't take away from the fact that it was very difficult for you."

Client: "Yeah."

Therapist: "Was there anyone in your life that was nurturing? A grandparent? A teacher? Anybody?"

Client: "My grandmother was mean, even to my mother. I suppose that's one reason my mother was as screwed up as she was."

Therapist: "That could have played a part in why your mom seems to have had such a difficult time. And I suppose her mother may have had things happen in her life that made her the way she was and so on."

Client: "Yes my grandmother grew up during the depression and had to raise her two younger brothers from the time she was about seven years old."

Therapist: "Yes. I suppose everyone does the best they can do with what they have to work with, but that doesn't take away from the fact that it was difficult growing up and you have some anger with your mother, and perhaps with your father, about that. What do you think you're most angry about when you think of your mother and the relationship you had with her?"

Client: "I don't know. I'm angry about so many things. I'm angry that she never did what she said she would do. I'm angry that she drank all the time. I'm angry she never stopped drinking and drank herself to death."

Therapist: "When you think about all those things you are angry about, what do you think causes you the most anger?"

Client: "I really don't know."

Therapist: "Well let's focus for a time on the fact that your mother wasn't trustworthy. She often didn't do what she promised you she would do. When you focus on this, how angry does it make you?"

Client: "Pretty angry."

Therapist: "On a scale of one to ten, if ten represents the most anger and one represents an absence of anger, where are you right now as you're thinking about the fact that your mother wasn't trustworthy and often let you down?"

Client: "Around a ten. It's really upsetting to me to think about this."

Therapist: " I know a technique that might help you with this. It might look a little strange to you at first. It's called Thought Field Therapy and it's based on the acupuncture or acupressure system. I've used it successfully with many clients and when it works it can be amazingly effective if you are willing to give it a try. It will involve you tapping on certain energy points while thinking about your anger. I would tap on my own body as we go along to demonstrate how it's done. You wouldn't even have to believe in it for it to work. It will either work or not work and doesn't take a long time to do, so you have nothing to lose. Want to give it a try?"

Client: "Okay. I'll do anything if it will help."

Therapist: "I think it has a good chance of helping. Let's give it a try. Before we get started are there any other feelings that you feel along with this anger, like sadness, for instance, or anxiety?"

Client: "No I just feel really angry."

Therapist: "Okay. I want you to keep focusing on your anger the whole time we do this exercise. This won't be about positive thinking. I want you to stay focused on the how angry you are at your mother and while you're focusing on your anger and it's about a ten, I want you to tap under your eye, right on the edge of the bony socket …."

Eventually, as your session or sessions progress, you and your client might find that you want to use Thought Field Therapy to address the client's anger about her mother's drinking and/or her mother's drinking herself to death. In this scenario, it is likely that sadness would come up. We might expect sadness about the fact that the mother could not be nurturing and wasted her life drinking. There might be sadness as well as anger around the fact that the mother is no longer alive and the grandchildren will never know their grandmother. Anger and sadness may eventually manifest itself around the father's abandonment.

While the typical and ordinary case proposed above would likely require several sessions to produce the client's stated goal of not feeling so angry all the time, there is a strong likelihood that Thought Field Therapy could dramatically reduce the client's level of anger in a very short period of time.

In the following chapters I will be presenting cases that will illustrate a variety of ways you can utilize TFT to make the good therapy you are already doing even better.

Chapter 3

Using Thought Field Therapy to Deal with Issues of Grief and Loss

"Emotions are negative when we react to them with grasping or aversion, because we then suffer from a constriction of consciousness. Emotions are negative to the extent we cling to them or flee from them."

Tenzing Wangyal Rinpoche

❖ ❖ ❖ ❖

To experience grief is inevitable. It is an inescapable part of our earthly cycle of life. As individuals we handle our grief in a variety of ways determined in part by family of origin, cultural identity, and religious or philosophical belief systems. But ultimately every individual handles his or her grief in his or her own unique way. As therapists it is to be expected that we encounter issues of grief and loss in our work with others as well as in our own lives.

Grieving is a natural process but often people feel unnaturally stuck in their grief or feel that the grief they are experiencing is more than they can bear. In addition, issues of anger or guilt frequently block a person's natural healing process. To be a therapist is to be an "expert" at helping our clients handle the grief they bring to their sessions. And yet we often feel helpless. We know that just listening, just being there, is of more value than we will ever know. We need to acknowledge our helplessness. We know that no one can bring back a loved one, nothing we say will fill that emptiness; that void will be there forever.

I believe our first task is to be comfortable with grief. To rush in and try to fix it before we are asked to "do something" may betray our own discomfort with loss and death. And yet, as helping professionals, we want to do something more to ease the pain, especially when our clients ask us to assist in their grieving process.

Some losses are obvious and others more subtle. All losses do not, of course, involve death. Besides death there are losses of health that we can help our clients mourn so that they can be more present in the life they do have. We help our clients mourn a difficult childhood so that they can have a happier adulthood. (I've never subscribed to the once popular belief that it's never too late to have a happy childhood. However I do believe it's never too late to have a happy adulthood.)

We help our clients who are getting a divorce not of their choosing to mourn this loss in their life so they can go forward and create or recreate a happier life. We help clients who are making a difficult decision to leave an abusive or alcoholic relationship grieve the loss of their fantasies and their dreams about what that relationship could have been. We help the adult child of a narcissistically impaired parent grieve the loss of their dream that that parent will ever give them what they want and need.

There is probably no area where the clinical use of TFT brings more relief of pain and suffering than in issues involving loss and grief.

Following are some case histories where I have combined Thought Field Therapy with more traditional ways of doing therapy to help a client move toward peace and acceptance.

Letting Go of Trying to Please a Narcissistically Impaired and Unavailable Parent

The stone cold reality hurt. I had just told Anne that she needed to accept the fact that she was never going to get what she wanted and needed from her mother. I told her as gently as possible that her mother was never going to tell her she loved her, or was proud of her, or thought she was a neat kid.

Now that she was a grown woman it was time for Anne to give up on the fantasy that if she only loved her mother enough, if she only worked for her mother hard enough, or if she could only figure out what her mother really wanted, someday her mother was going to approve of her, or compliment her, or support her, or love her in the way Anne wanted to be loved.

Our sessions together were to be about mourning and coming to terms with that loss.

When Anne first arrived at my office she told me that she was unhappy in her marital relationship and that she was having some thoughts about possibly ending her marriage. Sorting out her thoughts with a professional marriage and family therapist was Anne's explicitly expressed goal for these managed care sessions. However, there was another relationship in Anne's life that was troubling Anne even more than her relationship with her husband, and it soon became apparent that the implicit reason for Anne's visit was that she wanted help in figuring out what she could do to please this person. This person was Anne's mother.

As therapy progressed and Anne's story unfolded, the focus of our sessions became Anne's relationship with her difficult-to-please mother. Her problems with her mother turned out to be very much different from what Anne had originally supposed them to be. Anne's quandary was, quite simply, one of the most common ones encountered in traditional psychotherapy offices. "How can I please a person who can't be pleased?"

Anne had tried everything she knew how to do to get her mother's approval and she had secretly hoped that I could help her understand what she was "doing wrong."

It wasn't that Anne hadn't been a good kid growing up. Anne had received good grades in school, had done more than her share of household chores, and had never been in trouble at school. Anne had never gotten in trouble anywhere except in her own home, and at home Anne had always been in trouble.

During Anne's childhood years, her mother had doted on Anne's younger brother, Peter, but in her mother's eyes Anne could never get anything quite right. It seems that her mother lived in a divided world that was split into what Object Relation's Family Therapy would call a "good object" and a "bad object." Peter was, of course, the good object, and Anne, the bad. During Anne's childhood years, if Peter did something wrong, her mother would find a way to blame and punish Anne. Anne "should have been keeping an eye on Peter or he wouldn't have thrown that rock through a neighbor's window." Or, "Anne, should have carried the water to the dining room for Peter so he wouldn't have spilled it." No matter what she did, Anne had always been and still always was bad, wrong, stupid and inadequate in her mother's eyes.

Anne's mother had a successful career as an attorney, was president of the Parents and Teachers Association and active in her church. People would tell Anne that she was lucky to have such a devoted and talented mother. This made Anne even more certain that her mother was right and that something really was terribly wrong with her.

When Peter had received an A or even a B on his report card, it had been a cause for much celebration. Anne had regularly received As and Bs but her mother's only comments had been things like "Surely you could do better than this!", "What's this B in math about?", "Didn't you do your homework?", "You never were very good with numbers." And a disproportionate number of chores had been allocated to Anne who had to cook dinner, wash the dishes, put the dishes away, and take out the garbage before she was even allowed to do her homework, much less talk on the phone with a friend, watch television, or listen to music. Peter had no regular chores, and could watch television, listen to music, and play with his friends as he pleased.

Anne's father hadn't protected his daughter. When Anne's mother wasn't around, her weak and ineffectual father would pathetically try to make up for his lack of courage by giving Anne a special treat or taking her to a movie. Perhaps these gestures were as much for his benefit as for Anne's. Alone with his daughter, Anne's father likely felt the comfort one can feel when they are with someone who has suffered in a similar way. He too, had been verbally abused by Anne's mother. But Anne grew to despise her father for not standing up to his wife, either to defend her or himself.

Anne's father had often stood by helplessly as Anne was stuck at the receiving end of an hour-long verbally abusive tirade followed by a sentence of a month-long grounding from her mother. Her father would sometimes calmly sit as this abuse occurred, and read the paper as if nothing was going on.

When I first met Anne she was still trying to please her mother. Recently, after her mother had been diagnosed with cancer and was recovering from some related surgery, Anne had quit her job, temporarily left her husband and their two children and, for three months, had taken care of her mother who lived in a neighboring state. (By that time Anne's father was deceased.)

Anne's mother's gratitude was short lived. From her sick bed she managed to demean her tenacious and steadfastly determined-to-please daughter. She was sure that Anne "hadn't heard it right," and that she was "really supposed to take two capsules of her pain reliever a day not one." But then, Anne "never really did listen. Too bad that Peter couldn't be here at a time like this; he always knows the right thing to do," and so on. (In fact Peter, who lived quite close to his mother, had difficulty holding down a job, drank too much and had trouble getting his life to work for him.)

After her mother was somewhat restored to health, Anne returned to her family, exhausted and defeated. After all this, her mother was still not acknowledging what a "good kid" Anne was. Anne had, in fact, managed to return home only twice in the time she had been taking care of her mother. Anne had been, as was often the case, so busy being her mother's daughter that she didn't have much time to spend being herself, or the wife of her husband Mark, or the mother of her children. (In fact, as I spoke to Anne, it became clear that Mark did more than his share of caretaking, both of Anne and of the children. The children, I would soon discover, spent much of their time taking care of Anne.) Anne's unfinished business of childhood kept Anne from being an individuated and differentiated adult. Anne was still busy trying to be a good child.

I explained to Anne that her mother was, quite obviously, personality disordered. It is most likely that she would be diagnosed as a Narcissistic Personality Disorder. I double-checked my intuition about this by asking Anne a couple of key questions that I routinely ask when I suspect that a Narcissistic Personality Disorder plays a role in the dynamics of a relationship. I asked Anne: "Did your mother always have to be right? Did she ever admit to making mistakes? Do you remember her ever apologizing for anything? Did she have to be perfect and I mean PERFECT? Did she need to 'look good' at any cost?"

My intuition seemed to be validated by Anne's answers to these questions, and I explained that her mother needed Anne to be bad so that her mother could feel good. Her mother needed Anne to feel inadequate so that she could feel adequate, and her mother needed Anne to feel stupid so that she could feel smart. And she needed Anne to be wrong so that she could be right.

The seriously narcissistically impaired are like black holes. Their needs for a narcissistic supply of power and attention can suck the very life out of those who are close to them. And it is frequently difficult for those who are in a relationship with them to find the power to escape their grasp.

In the past, when Anne would get tired of her mother's maltreatment of her, she would eventually withdraw. Her mother would quickly lure Anne back with sweetness and half-hearted apologies. She needed Anne to stay in the position of (in the language of Object Relations Theory) the "bad object" and she needed Anne to be an "object" on which to project her own unconscious fears about her inner self.

I explained to Anne that deep down it is likely that her mother felt inadequate, bad, undeserving and stupid. But those deeply buried feelings were not available in any conscious way to Anne's mother. Her mother dealt with this intra-psychic material by projecting it onto Anne. I further explained, that most of us feel these kinds of fears from time to time. Occasionally we may feel insecure or unworthy or suffer some other anxiety about ourselves. However, most of us are conscious of these fears when we have them, which make these feelings of insecurity, unworthiness or un-deservedness easier problems to work with.

The Narcissistic Personality Disordered person is not aware of any of these feelings. They avoid feeling these deeply buried feelings at any and all cost. If they were to enter into this space and feel their pain, it would simply be too much for them to bear, so they avoid looking at themselves. They use the psychological defense of projecting and they see in others the shortcomings they are unable to see in themselves.

The Narcissist is, of course, self focused, so they will see others as being selfish, when they don't want to do exactly what the narcissistically impaired person wants them to do. They need those close to them to think exactly as they do. They cannot understand that people close to them can agree to disagree. They cannot take the chance of being wrong, so those close to them must validate the truth of the Narcissist's reality and agree with them on just about everything.

The narcissistically impaired are not tolerant of even a shade of criticism. To them, a differing opinion that is vocalized by one who is close to them feels like intense criticism. This difference of opinion can frequently be a trigger that sends the narcissistically impaired person into a narcissistic rage. The narcissistic rage is a kind of adult temper tantrum. The narcissist works on the theory that a good offense is the best defense. Despite being in an adult body and perhaps, as is often the case, even being very accomplished and skilled in the outside world, the narcissistically impaired person is tragically stunted emotionally. They are children in an adult body and frequently behave emotionally as would a very young child.

I explained to Anne, that it wasn't that her mother didn't love her. Her mother did love her to the best of her ability. But her mother was severely limited in her capacity to love anyone. Anne's mother saw the world as her oyster. She lacked the ability to empathize with others. She saw Anne, Anne's father and Peter as extensions of herself.

Anne's mother may have appeared to connect with others at times, but this was for the purpose of looking good.

I explained to Anne that high functioning Narcissistic Personality Disordered persons excel at looking good. Narcissistically impaired people need a constant "narcissistic supply" of recognition, compliments and praise. They often enter professions that have high social status, and achieve political positions in an effort to maintain their narcissistic supply of praise and recognition. This praise and recognition serves as a psychological defense and keeps them from feeling the feelings of shame and inadequacy buried deep inside of them. This praise and recognition, often so successfully achieved by the highly functioning narcissistically impaired, also makes for all the more confusion on the part of those who are close to them. "If all these people think my mother (or my father or my husband) is so wonderful, the problem must be me."

It should be mentioned that, although Anne's mother seemingly was a highly functioning, severely narcissistically impaired person, not all seriously narcissistically impaired people are as successful at looking good. Although Anne's mother successfully hid her impairment from most of the outside world, some lower functioning Narcissistic Personality Disordered people are not so adept at hiding their limitations.

Well hidden or not so well hidden, the dynamics are similar. Narcissistic Personality disordered people have to be perfect. To them, the other person, if not in complete agreement with them, is always wrong. They take the act of questioning them as severe criticism and this predictably triggers rage. They definitely don't live by the "golden rule" of "doing to others as you would have them do to you." The rules are different for them than for others. And although some conceal it better than others, they lack the ability to empathize, the ability to get inside of someone else's skin and see things from another's perspective. Rather, they see others as an extension of themselves. And they lack an ability to objectively look at themselves.

I explained to Anne that she and her mother had an implicit agreement and I would like to help make it explicit. She and her mother had both agreed that Anne's mother's wants and needs were more important than Anne's wants and needs. They had continued working under this contract for over thirty years. I asked Anne if she wanted to break this contract and begin to take care of herself. To do this she was going to have to give up her futile attempts to gain her mother's love and approval. Anne then asked the inevitable question and wondered aloud if, with therapy, could her mother change?

Anne needed to know that when the severely narcissistically impaired come to therapy, it is most frequently to talk about how to fix someone else. The Narcissist wants our collaboration in fixing the other person who they genuinely believe needs fixing. They are difficult clients because they are so exquisitely defended and so exquisitely sensitive to any suggestion that they might not be perfect. I very much doubted if Anne's mother would entertain the idea of therapy. Anne acknowledged that her mother didn't believe in therapy and thought that therapy usually made things worse.

Her mother had said, "People go to therapy and blame their parents for everything." and "It's always the parents' fault." I could recognize Anne's mother's hidden fears and I also recognized Anne's fear that I would ask her to sever her relationship with her mother. This would not be the case.

I told Anne that I personally believe that people do the best they can do at the time, considering what has happened to them in the past, considering the knowledge that they've been exposed to, and considering their genetic limitations and capabilities. I have no way to know if this is true or not, but it's not up to me to judge and I always try to operate without blame. This is different than believing people shouldn't be held responsible and accountable for their actions. And it does not get in the way of empathizing with someone who has suffered at the hands of another, no matter the reason the other was so limited, damaged or impaired.

On one hand, Anne felt a sense of relief when she understood that her mother's limitations, and not her own limitations, were at the core of her mother's absence of nurturing and support and frequently cruel ways of dealing with Anne. On the other hand, Anne now felt an intense wave of deep existential sadness and grief.

If I could have told Anne that she could do something clever and different, she could have been more hopeful of gaining her mother's love and approval. However, with her new understanding of her mother's limitations, Anne became painfully aware that there was really nothing she could do to gain her mother's love. Their painful relationship had always been about her mother's limitations and not about Anne's.

We were now at the point where this narrative began and Anne was facing this truth. Her mother would never love her in the way she wanted her mother to love her. Anne was sobbing uncontrollably. I asked Anne if she would like to grieve this loss, have peace and acceptance around her mother's limitations, and learn new ways to relate to her mother that were healthier for her? Anne nodded her head in agreement and asked, "But how?" I asked Anne if she would like to try Thought Field Therapy.

We used the Thought Field Therapy grief/anxiety/anger algorithm and Anne soon reported peace and acceptance around her mother's limitations.

Anne next reported a feeling of anger around her father's ineffectualness and lack of protection of her. Only after dealing with her grief around her connection with her mother was Anne able to realize just how angry she still was with her father. I reminded Anne that in putting up with her mother's verbal abuse she had become somewhat like him. Perhaps this is one reason she felt so angry. I assumed the possibility of grief and anxiety here also, and to be on the safe side, I again led Anne through the grief/anxiety/anger algorithm. This time, Anne stayed focused on the feelings of anger toward her father. Again, after completing the treatment, Anne reported a feeling of peace and acceptance.

The following week, I asked Anne how it was going and if she had noticed anything different, either for the better or for the worse. She reported that she had had one conversation on the phone with her mother. It had not gone well. Her mother complained about everything including the fact that, after all she "had done for her children," she "just couldn't depend on anyone to help" her. She just had "to do everything" herself. It had "always" been that way.

I asked Anne, how her mother's complaints had affected her. Anne had to stop and think. Anne seemed surprised when she remembered that she had not been upset by her mother's comments and had not felt compelled to give up living her own life in an effort to rescue her mother. This was a much different response than Anne would have had previous to doing the Thought Field Therapy and Anne realized how much work she had accomplished during her previous session.

However, Anne had made the mistake of trying to explain to her mother why she could no longer be away from home to help her. Anne commented that defending her decision in this way really hadn't helped. She had gotten nowhere with her mother by attempting to reason with her.

I instructed Anne that lesson number one when dealing with someone like her mother was, paradoxically,"Don't defend yourself." Although this notion is counter-intuitive, it is the one method that I find works when dealing with a person who is severely narcissistically impaired.

For as long as Anne could remember, she had been reasoning with her mother in an effort to get her mother to see her as a person with her own reality and her own point of view. This works when you are dealing with someone who is coming from a rational place and with someone who has the emotional capacity to put herself or himself in the reality of another person in an attempt to understand them and empathize with them. But Anne's mother was not coming from a rational place and Anne's mother did not have the emotional capacity to empathize. Instead, Anne's mother's goal was one of emotional survival, which required her to project her own fears of inadequacy on someone else, which usually turned out to be Anne.

Anne had to learn to say things to her mother like, "I can hear that you really need help." and "I know you wish I could be there." And, she would need to learn how to attempt to change the subject. She would need to learn to say things like, "That's an interesting way to look at it. I look at it differently but we can agree to disagree." or "I can see how you're looking at it. I don't look at it the same way, but that's okay." She would need to persist and not get hooked into defending herself. We would later practice these techniques in our therapy sessions.

Anne eventually had to tell her mother that if her mother continued to personally attack her, Anne would be forced to hang up the phone. She gave her mother a choice. "You talk to me respectfully or you are choosing to be hung up on."

Anne's mother slowly learned to speak to Anne without making negative personal comments about Anne. Anne had unilaterally written a new contract and, under the terms of this new contract, Anne's needs and wants would be equally important.

In another session, we approached the subject of Anne's younger brother, Peter. As mentioned earlier, Peter was drinking heavily and not doing well. Anne was feeling anger around her brother's easier life. Anne's mother still enabled Peter financially and he continued to be his mother's favorite child and her confidant.

I pointed out to Anne that she actually had the better position even though it could not have seemed like it at the time she was growing up. By trying hard to please her mother, she had learned to be helpful to others, conscientious, and hard working. She had learned to be empathetic and aware. While Anne may have learned these things too well, to the exclusion of learning to take care of her own needs, she was now learning to take care of herself.

Learning to take care of oneself is an easy task, compared to the task of learning to be aware of and to be conscious of the needs of others. As a child, and continuing into adulthood, little had been expected of Peter. He never had the opportunity to develop the protective factors of initiative and self-control. He never learned to develop a tolerance for frustration and to delay gratification for greater rewards down the road. And, Peter was suffering greatly as the result. Peter could not keep a job and drank heavily to dull the pain of his failure.

We used the anger algorithm to address Anne's anger with her brother, which, after the above conversation, had been reduced to a SUD level of four. Using Thought Field Therapy, Anne's anger at her brother was quickly reduced to a one.

Anne was doing better now that she was accepting her mother's severe limitations. She was, at the same time, taking better care of herself by refusing to accept her mother's abuse. It was finally time to re-visit the problem that initially brought Anne to treatment—her relationship with her husband.

It sounded from the start that Anne's husband, Mark, did many things right. According to Anne, Mark was helpful with the children; he was a good father and their children adored him. When Anne had gone to take care of her mother, Mark had supported Anne by assuming full responsibility for the children, for paying bills, and for keeping up the house and yard. Mark actually sounded too good to be true. There was, of course, more to the story.

Although Anne had, in the past, been much like her father when it came to acquiescing to her mother, I wondered if perhaps she was somewhat different with Mark. Perhaps Mark tried too hard to take care of Anne and he didn't take care of himself. Or, I wondered, perhaps Anne might have married her mother in a kind of repetition compulsion. Maybe there was some lack of ability to empathize on Mark's part; Anne had found someone like her mother and was trying to get from him what she couldn't get from her mother.

It was my first guess that was, in actuality, the closest to the truth. Mark tried hard to please Anne and Anne took advantage of it. It did seem like Mark was not as good at taking care of himself as he was of taking care of others and that Anne had great voids that needed to be filled. I explained to Anne that no other person could ever fill these voids and that she needed to learn to stand on her own two feet.

No matter how hard he tried, Mark could not make up for the lack of nurturing and support Anne had experienced in her childhood. Mark undoubtedly needed to understand this also. Perhaps Anne could suggest to Mark that he do some individual therapy on his own, and later, hopefully, she and Mark might think about doing some short term couple therapy.

For now, I suggested that Anne might want to concentrate on working on herself. Anne agreed that she needed to lower her expectations of Mark and raise her expectations about what she could do for herself.

In our last two sessions we used Thought Field Therapy to address Anne's issues of self-esteem.

We began with Anne focusing on her feelings of being unlovable. Already doing somewhat better cognitively with this issue, Anne was still stuck emotionally with feelings of "un-lovability." She quickly went from a SUD of eight to a SUD of one while doing the grief/anxiety algorithm. (I chose grief/anxiety as these feelings had to do with hurts from the past and anxiety around her lovability in the present and future. Working with issues of self-esteem is covered in more detail in Chapter 5.)

We worked on Anne's feelings of being inadequate or "stupid" in much the same way. Using the Thought Field Therapy grief/anxiety algorithm these feelings were also reduced, this time from a SUD level of six to SUD level of one.

I believed that there were still dynamics in Anne's relationship with her husband that would need to be addressed in the future. As Anne became less her mother's child and more a differentiated adult this would likely shift Ann's and Mark's relationship structure. Anne had already found herself being more present and interested in their two children now that she was not so busy trying to please her mother, and Anne was no longer so unhappy with Mark that she was considering the possibility of divorcing him.

Mark would have to learn how to take better care of himself in the relationship and not be as focused on pleasing Anne. I had a feeling that Anne would actually be more pleased with Mark if he stopped trying so hard to please her and also worked on becoming a more self-differentiated person. Perhaps they would need further help from a professional at some point or perhaps these changes would continue to evolve as the couple communicated in a more direct and adult way.

In eight sessions, Anne was able to grieve the loss of the fantasy that her mother would ever be who she wanted and needed her to be. She began to deal more realistically with her mother and began taking better care of herself. Although Anne's brother Peter was still the "favorite one," Anne no longer thought of her brother as the "lucky one."

Anne was becoming and behaving like a more self-differentiated adult; she was more realistic in her expectations of her husband and was no longer reporting feelings of being unlovable or inadequate.

Anne's Thought Field Therapy Recipes

Grief/Anxiety/Anger:
Eyebrow, eye, arm, collarbone, little finger, collarbone
9-Gamut Treatment
Eyebrow, eye, arm, collarbone, little finger, collarbone

Anger:
Little finger, collarbone
9-Gamut Treatment
Little finger, collarbone

Grief/Anxiety:
Eyebrow, eye, arm, collarbone
9-Gamut Treatment
Eyebrow, eye, arm, collarbone

Feelings of Loss Around a Lost Relationship and a Lost Childhood (When the Childhood Memories Are Not Available Consciously)

Helen was in tears even before she entered my office. She had taken the day off from her job at a local hospital where she was employed as a nurse. Helen sobbed that she had been in a three-year "relationship from Hell." Tears continued to well up in her dark brown eyes and stream down her face as she related her story. Dirk had been unconfident and shy when he and Helen first met. Helen, a natural caretaker, had coached Dirk for a period of time and he eventually grew confident enough, at Helen's suggestion, to enter therapy.

Eventually Dirk had become so "confident" that he began dating other women. Helen was devastated but at the same time stated that she didn't really want Dirk back. Helen had had plenty of therapy in the past and stated that she was not interested, at this time, in long-term therapy. She was looking for help and wanted help fast. I told Helen that I had a method of doing therapy that was sometimes successful in accomplishing therapy goals in a very short time. I couldn't guarantee any results, but if she was willing to try an unusual but effective technique, we could give it a try.

Intellectually, Helen knew that Dirk wasn't good for her, but at the same time she had difficulty getting over him. During our first session we dove in and addressed Helen's grief around the fact that her relationship with Dirk didn't work out. Helen's SUD level of nine was quickly lowered to a one after doing just the simple grief algorithm. As is my custom, I asked Helen to "scan this problem" by imagining various scenarios which might have brought up these feelings of loss and sadness in the past. If there was still some aspect of this problem that brought up unwanted feelings, we needed to know so we could work on it.

Helen did think of a situation that caused her anxiety to go up to a nine just imagining it. Even though she was clear that she didn't want Dirk back again, Helen was filled with anxiety and sadness when she imagined seeing Dirk with another woman. Although Helen lived in a large city, she and Dirk lived in the same apartment complex and it was likely that such a sighting could happen sometime in the future.

This time we used the combined anxiety/grief algorithm and Helen soon reported feeling no anxiousness around the prospect of seeing Dirk with another woman. Helen stated that she felt "tons lighter" and that she wanted to work on another problem next week if this treatment "held up."

At the beginning of the second session Helen reported that she had little sadness around the fact that her relationship with Dirk had ended. She hadn't as yet seen him out in public, alone or with another woman. However, she thought that if she saw Dirk with another woman, she would "just feel sorry for the other woman."

Helen had some very mixed feelings about what she wanted to work on next. Helen was unusual in that she had little memory of her childhood before the age of twelve. Previous therapists had suspected that she had been sexually abused in her childhood. Two flashbacks that Helen had experienced during recent years led some credibility to this suspicion. In addition, she had relayed her suspicions to her mother and her mother thought that it was quite likely that these events had occurred. At any rate, Helen stayed away from thinking or experiencing feelings connected to her mysterious childhood because of the terror and anger that overwhelmed her when she attempted to revisit this period of her life.

In the office, Helen agreed to think about this missing period of her life. While she experienced no memories in the form of pictures or sounds, she was experiencing intense feelings of terror and anger. Helen was sobbing uncontrollably. We did the grief/anxiety/anger algorithm and her SUD level was finally down to a one as far as the anxiety and the feelings of grief and terror. But Helen's anger level had risen even higher, she reported, than when we had initially begun.

Helen was no longer sobbing, but she was hardly breathing as we focused on her anger. This time, using the anger algorithm alone, we brought Helen's SUD level down to a one. Helen stated that she couldn't remember ever feeling as "light." She described it as "feeling like my chest is empty and full of air and that it is filling up with happiness."

Helen was not interested in "recovering" her memories. She knew that, in all likelihood, some bad things had happened to her, and now, free of her terror and anger, she had a pretty good idea about what had happened. However, Helen didn't want her past to define who she was today. She wanted to go on with her life.

She was now ready to talk about how she could take better care of herself today and in the future. She wanted to get out of her old familiar caretaker role. As we talked, I related to her that, in my experience, women (and men) who have been sexually abused tend to want to be in control. During his or her childhood they were not in control, and they often see the world in terms of "either you're in control or someone is controlling you." They need to learn about a third way where each partner is equal and neither is trying to control the other.

Women and men who have been sexually abused are often attracted to passive, ineffectual, dependent partners as a way of staying in control. It feels safe. They need to learn to look for people whose lives are "up and running," people who aren't looking for someone to take care of them and who don't need to be "fixed." Our third and last session consisted of talking about just these things.

Many clients begin remembering more about their past during the process of doing Thought Field Therapy. In Helen's case, this was not her goal. I don't know if Helen is remembering her childhood at this time in her life or not.

In the past we, as therapists, emphasized "remembering," sometimes in great detail, as a way of helping clients go on with their future free of negative baggage from the past. Helen may come back for more help some time in the future, but I am reasonably confident that the work we did during these three sessions helped Helen move toward a healthier and happier life despite her lack of "recovered memories."

Helen's story illustrates how TFT can work on memories that aren't there in the usual form that memories take. That is, they are not present as a snapshot, or a movie, or as sound bites. Her story illustrates how TFT can assist in a client's recovery without needing to "recapture" pictorial or audio memories.

Helen's second treatment also contains an example of "Tooth-Shoe-Lump" (The TFT term for working through the layers of a problem as they arise. Please see the FAQ chapter for a more thorough explanation of this term.) In this case, the anger treatment spot was included in the first treatment; however, Helen's thought field likely wasn't tuned in to the anger at the beginning of that treatment. Thus, the anger needed to be addressed separately as a second algorithm, after the grief and anxiety (terror) had subsided.

Helen's Thought Field Therapy Recipes

Grief/Anxiety/Anger
Eyebrow, eye, arm, collarbone, little finger, collarbone
9-Gamut Treatment
Eyebrow, eye, arm, collarbone, little finger, collarbone.

Anger
Little finger, collarbone
9-Gamut Treatment
Little finger, collarbone

Reducing the Feelings of Grief,Guilt and Anger When the Loss Is Recent, Catastrophic and Traumatic

There is no greater loss than the loss of a child, unless perhaps it is the loss of an only child or the loss of a child who is murdered in a senseless and cruel way. Grace's only son was the victim of a cruel and brutal gang murder. He had been beaten to death. To make things worse, if that were possible, Grace was feeling guilt around having sent her son Eddie to live with friends on the East Coast because she had felt that the 17-year-old boy was running around with the wrong crowd. Eddie had been getting more and more involved with drugs, and Grace felt that getting away from his old friends and spending time with these friends would be good for her son.

When Grace first came to therapy, she felt stuck with memories of Eddie as he lay in a hospital bed, tubes protruding from his body and his head grossly deformed by the beating that left him comatose and which, before the night was over, took his life. Her realization that Eddie must have died a terrifying death blotted out her entire memory of Eddie's short but, for the most part, happy life. Grace could not remember the good times they had shared, the closeness that they had enjoyed for so many years, or the many talents and the kindness that was so much a part of who Eddie was. Only this one terrifying and brutal memory seemed to remain. It is important to note that I did not ask Grace if she wanted to get over the grief she felt around her son's death.

It is common for those who have lost a loved one to feel that their grief is the one thing that keeps them connected to the their lost loved one. To let go of that grief would mean that their loved one would really be gone and that they were now really alone. Grief is one way to feel connected. Additionally, it is common for people who are grieving to feel like they would be minimizing their loss, or they would be being unfaithful to a loved ones memory or they would be dishonoring the departed loved one's importance in their lives, if they were not in mourning.

So, of course, I would never ask a client this early in their grief if they wanted to be over their grief. Instead, I asked Grace if she would like to diminish the power of this last memory of her son. Perhaps then, I suggested, she might be able to feel more connected to Eddie through their happier memories; when they were together, laughing and celebrating, and sometimes crying, through the large and small events that shaped their lives.

Of course, Grace wanted to be connected to her son's memory in a positive way. We used the grief/anxiety algorithm and in that session the memory of Grace's last moments with Eddie faded. She smiled and asked me if she had mentioned how funny Eddie was.

During Grace's second session she was, of course, still grieving the tremendous loss she had experienced. She was also having intense feelings of guilt around sending Eddie to live on the East Coast. Grace and I engaged in Cognitive Therapy. I reminded her that her intentions had been good. She hadn't had a crystal ball and couldn't possibly have predicted the future. I reminded her that we all make great Monday morning quarterbacks.

While Grace agreed with me that these arguments all made perfectly good sense, she felt no less guilty. Her right brain and her left-brain were not connecting on this one. We agreed to use Thought Field Therapy in an attempt to reduce the feelings of guilt that Grace was experiencing around her son's death. To be on the safe side, I utilized an algorithm using the past trauma/grief treatment, the anxiety treatment and the guilt treatment. When Grace focused on her feelings of guilt she reported a SUD level of "twenty" on a scale of one to ten. After completing the treatment, Grace reported a SUD level of one.

In Grace's case, the loss was so fresh that various layers of guilt and grief came up during the course of her treatment. In each case, Thought Field Therapy was able to at least reduce some of her pain and suffering. In Grace's case our therapy was not especially brief therapy and my support during this period of Grace's life, I have no doubt, was just as important as the use of Thought Field Therapy. This was a case where Thought Field Therapy was combined with Support Therapy, each therapy enhancing the other.

Issues of anger came up as therapy progressed. Anger at Eddie's father for not ever having been there for Eddie. Anger at the gang members, (some who had been apprehended and some who by then had real names and faces). In each case the Thought Field Therapy interventions were successful in that they brought some immediate and lasting relief.

After completing her course of treatment, Grace came back for a session to deal with the anxiety she was feeling about being present for the trial of Eddie's killers. We were able to reduce her anxiety while thinking about this experience in the office. Later Grace wrote to me and let me know that the trial had gone the way she had hoped. Although sitting through the trial was difficult, she remained rational and at peace.

Grace's story illustrates how one can work with grief that is recent, and, it illustrates how one can combine Support Therapy with Thought Field Therapy.

Grace's Thought Field Therapy Recipes

Grief/Anxiety:
Eyebrow, eye, arm, collarbone
9-Gamut Treatment
Eyebrow, eye, arm, collarbone

Grief/Anxiety/Guilt:
Eyebrow, eye, arm, collarbone, index finger, collarbone
9-Gamut Treatment
Eyebrow, eye, arm, collarbone, index finger, collarbone

Grief/Anxiety/Anger:
Eyebrow, eye, arm, collarbone, little finger, collarbone
9-Gamut Treatment
Eyebrow, eye, arm, collarbone, little finger, collarbone

Chapter 4

Using Thought Field Therapy in an Anger Management Program

You will see that forgiveness is fundamentally for your own sake, a way to carry the pain of the past no longer.

Jack Kornfield, *A Path With a Heart*

❖ ❖ ❖ ❖

Using the TFT Treatment for Many Layers of Anger with a Person Who Is Seriously Mentally Ill and Who Suffers from Food Sensitivities

In the past I received many referrals from an intensive probation program whose mission was preventing individuals in the program from returning to prison or jail. Most frequently they were referred to me for anger management.

It is important to note that while anger management implies that clients of such a program will learn to control their anger, Thought Field Therapy, by removing the perturbations from the client's thought field, eliminates their anger as opposed to controlling it.

Daphne was on intense probation. She had been diagnosed as bipolar and schizophrenic. She also suffered from epilepsy. She was taking several medications in an apparently successful effort to address these problems and she presented as bright and appropriate. Daphne was 40 years old and had three children who were living with their father in another state.

I began by letting Daphne know that she had been referred to me because her probation officer thought she had issues with anger. I asked Daphne if she was indeed angry. Daphne acknowledged that she was currently angry and upset because she was not allowed to visit her boyfriend who was in prison at the time. She missed him and was angry with her probation officer for not allowing her to see him.

Her boyfriend James was in prison for domestic violence. Daphne had several times been his victim and Daphne had suffered broken ribs, a black eye and swollen lips as a result of these beatings. But this had "only been when James had been drinking" Daphne said. She was devoted to him and felt that because of his experience in prison James had really changed.

Toward the end of our first session, Daphne stated her treatment goals. Daphne wanted to be less angry and she also wanted to have less pain in her right hand on the little finger side (which, coincidentally or not, is the location of the heart meridian treatment spot, the one we frequently use in Thought Field Therapy when treating anger).

During Daphne's second session we talked about her history. Daphne had been married for 20 years to a man who had, according to Daphne, ignored her and was hardly ever home. Sadly, after Daphne divorced this man, he changed jobs and stayed home. Daphne had been with James, her current boyfriend, for five years.

Daphne's father, an alcoholic, had been physically, sexually and emotionally abusive. He began sexually abusing Daphne when she was 12 years old. He began sexually abusing Daphne's younger sister when her sister was age three. At age 16 Daphne had had enough and after threatening her father's life she left home. To the best of Daphne's knowledge her father never abused her younger sister after this confrontation. Later, after she was married and had borne children, Daphne and her sister broke their silence and told their mother about the sexual abuse, but their mother, according to Daphne, never believed that this had really happened.

Daphne stated that she was still angry with her father but wanted to forgive him. She said that she wanted to be more in touch with the love that she had held for her father. We agreed to work on this anger toward her former perpetrator during next week's session.

During her next session, as Daphne had requested, we began working on Daphne's justifiable but unwanted anger towards her father. The simple grief/anxiety/ anger algorithm brought Daphne's SUD level down to a one. Daphne then reported that she was now conscious of some feelings of guilt about the fact that she was glad that her father was dead. (Daphne's father had passed away many years previously.) We successfully addressed this by using the guilt algorithm.

During this session, Daphne reported feeling more at peace about her father. She commented that she had a feeling that he too, was more at peace. I helped Daphne understand that she had had no reason to feel guilty because she was happy that her father was dead. I told her that it was perfectly natural to experience relief at not having to deal with her father after what had happened in the past. At the end of the session, Daphne was not feeling anger toward her deceased father and she was no longer feeling guilty for being glad that he was dead.

Daphne came in for her fifth session focused on an upsetting memory that frequently intruded into her daily life. This intrusive memory or unwanted thought had to do with the first time she was molested by her father. This time the treatment unfortunately wasn't so easy. We used the trauma/anxiety/anger algorithm and it just wasn't working. After doing the psychological reversal correction, the recurring psychological reversal, we were still getting nowhere and Daphne was still stuck at a SUD level of ten, thinking about this terrifying and traumatic event in her life. Finally I remembered to try Collarbone Breathing. After doing the Collarbone Breathing Technique, Daphne was able to respond to the trauma/anxiety/anger algorithm treatment and was soon reporting a SUD level of one while thinking about this horrific event.

During this same session another issue involving feelings of guilt surfaced. Daphne remembered her last day living at her parent's home when, after an especially severe beating from her father she had said, "If you touch me again, I'll kill you!"

Daphne was smart enough to know that she had every right to say what she had said and she also knew that the words she had uttered had protected both her and her sister from further abuse. But still Daphne felt guilty and rated her feelings of guilt at a seven on the SUD scale. By doing the guilt algorithm once again, Daphne's SUD level went down to a one.

During her next session Daphne reported having no anger or other negative feelings about the past and she reported amazement that the "tapping treatment" had worked.

In the following weeks, we successfully worked on Daphne's anger at her probation officer, an anger that wasn't helping Daphne in her efforts to get permission to visit her boyfriend. We also worked successfully on her fear of crowds and her fear of public places. The pain in her hand that Daphne had mentioned in her first session gradually disappeared.

Daphne had mentioned the possibility that she might be suffering from food sensitivities. Daphne not only suffered from epilepsy but she reported that she frequently suffered from severe migraine headaches and that she felt constantly tired.

Having been trained in TFT at the Causal Diagnostic level, I was able to test Daphne for possible individual energy toxins using an advanced form of muscle testing developed by Dr. Roger Callahan. (If you are not trained at the diagnostic level, you may need to refer your client to a therapist who is trained at this more advanced level of TFT in an effort to get at the root cause of physical problems, such as migraine headaches and occasionally even the brain misfiring that occurs with epilepsy.) In Daphne's case it was confirmed through muscle testing that Daphne was indeed sensitive to dairy products.

As another way to help Daphne identify possible dietary sensitivities, I introduced Daphne to the Pulse Test, a test developed by the allergy specialist Arthur F. Coca, MD[1]. This test was designed by Dr. Coca as a tool to assist people who suspect they might suffer from food and or environmental sensitivities in identifying foods or other substances that might possibly be harmful or troublesome for them. When the possibilities are identified, a traditional elimination diet can be utilized.

The simple theory behind Dr. Coca's test is that when a person ingests a food that is not harmonious for them, or when a person breathes a substance that is not harmonious for them, the pulse rate will increase significantly above its normal level. In Daphne's case, she found that when she ate anything containing any form of dairy, her pulse was elevated from the low 60s (BPM) to over 80 (BPM) within thirty minutes. So, Daphne received some validation for the notion of a possible dairy sensitivity from the Pulse Test as well. (It is important to note that in many cases clients could be sensitive, as an example, to milk, sour cream and yogurt but not to certain cheeses. Daphne just happened to be sensitive to all dairy products that we tested. It is important to test for specific foods rather than general food categories, such as dairy, or soy, or vegetables.)

Eliminating dairy would not be an easy thing to ask Daphne to do. In fact, Daphne practically lived on dairy. As is often the case with troublesome foods, Daphne craved dairy products and ate them daily, sometimes as often as three times a day.

However, after doing the pulse test, Daphne was convinced to give it a try, and for a week she eliminated dairy from her diet. The next week, Daphne reported that, since eliminating all dairy products, she had not had any headaches. And she was no longer feeling constantly tired.

It was Daphne's eleventh session and she was preparing to attend her boyfriend's parole hearing. Daphne was concerned that she would be too anxious and that she might say the wrong thing if she were asked questions. Her current anxiety went from a seven to a one with the anxiety algorithm and I gave Daphne a take-home version of the algorithm so she could repeat it at any time if needed.

The next week Daphne sadly reported that her boyfriend's parole had been denied. However, a bright spot was that she had not been anxious when answering questions before the parole board. Daphne also reported feeling much less tired and not having experienced any migraine headaches since eliminating the dairy products. Daphne's twelve allotted sessions had now been used and we terminated our treatment. However, four months later, Daphne's probation officer allowed her to come in for three additional sessions. These sessions had to do with preparing Daphne for James' release from prison.

When I saw Daphne four months later she expressed frustration that her boyfriend would be in a halfway house for the next sixth months. I helped her look at the positive side. James would be getting help and she would get to see him when she could arrange a trip to visit him during visiting hours. Eventually, if all went well, they would have weekend visits and, most important of all, in the meantime Daphne would be safe.

During the following visit we used TFT to address Daphne's frustration. I usually assume that frustration is a low level anxiety mixed with some anger. So we used the "frustration" algorithm, or the anxiety/anger algorithm, and Daphne's level of frustration was reduced to a one or a two. Because Daphne wasn't working and needed to take her focus off of James, I suggested that she go to the library and get a library card, pick out a book, and perhaps ask about literacy classes for herself. This might add some interest to her life and help her make good use of her excess time. We talked about her going back to work once again and possibly getting off of disability. To do this Daphne would need to take her CNA training over again and pass a test. She agreed to consider this option.

When I saw Daphne for her final session a month later, she had good news. She had scored 98% on her CNA exam and had graduated at the top of her class. She had graduated Magna Cum Laude and was the class Valedictorian. She reported that she was now feeling encouraged to go even further in her career.

Daphne would soon be able to see James every other weekend. She was no longer tired or experiencing headaches now that she had, except for rare occasions, eliminated dairy. Most important of all, Daphne was seeing the wisdom of James being in a program where there would be a third party involved in making his transition from prison back to everyday life.

Daphne's story provides an example of using Thought Field Therapy while working with a person who has a serious mental illness that is being controlled, in part, by medication. It also illustrates the many layers of anger that can be addressed using Thought Field Therapy. It is worthwhile to note that only after using the Collarbone Breathing in Daphne's fifth session did the algorithm I had selected to address her trauma finally work. And if not for identifying the fact that dairy was troublesome in Daphne's life,

Daphne would likely have been too tired and too limited by her migraines to have ever returned to work.

Daphne's Thought Field Therapy Recipes:

Grief/Anxiety/Anger
Eyebrow, eye, arm, collarbone, little finger, collarbone
9-Gamut Treatment
Eyebrow, eye, arm, collarbone, little finger, collarbone

Guilt
Index finger, collarbone
9-Gamut Treatment
Index finger, collarbone

Anxiety/Phobia
Eye, arm, collarbone
9-Gamut Treatment
Eye, arm, collarbone

Frustration (Anxiety/Anger)
Eye, arm, collarbone, little finger, collarbone
9-Gamut Treatment
Eye, arm, collarbone, little finger, collarbone

Using TFT When The Anger You're Dealing with Is an Issue of Transference

Eduardo, a strikingly handsome Latino, was employed as a project manager for a large construction company. Eduardo was not on probation, but had been referred by the court to my "anger management program". He had waited for several weeks to make an appointment and now his time for completing this court-ordered program was down to the wire. Three months prior to his visit, Eduardo had pushed and shoved his wife Tanya and pinned her against a wall. When Tanya finally freed herself, she called the police and reported Eduardo's abuse. Eduardo spent a night in jail and was released on bail the following morning. Eduardo was required to complete an anger management program consisting of a minimum of ten sessions.

Eduardo readily admitted that he was frequently verbally abusive to Tanya, his second wife. Tanya and Eduardo had been married almost ten years. Eduardo's first wife, the mother of his children, had divorced him many years ago due to Eduardo's verbal and physical abuse. Eduardo hung his head as he acknowledged that this was not the first time he had pushed and shoved his wife to the point of leaving bruises on her wrists and arms. He seemed to be feeling genuine remorse but at the same time feeling hopeless concerning his ability to change. Eduardo reported that he hadn't been able to figure out what he could do to control these angry outbursts. They seemed to him to come from nowhere. He had begun to accept that this was, in his words, "just the way I am put together."

This most recent incident of domestic violence, the one that Tanya had reported, had taken place while Tanya was recovering from a brief illness. She had been bedridden for several days. Eduardo was not aware of anything that might have triggered his violence.

I was beginning to form the usual hypothesis. I wondered if perhaps Eduardo was used to being waited on and if he had been growing intolerant of having to do things for himself during Tanya's brief illness. Not only might he have had to take care of himself during Tanya's illness, I imagined, but he may have had to take care of Tanya as well. If Eduardo had feelings of entitlement this may have been too much for him to handle and he had finally exploded. If this were the case we would have to address Eduardo's feelings of entitlement.

However, it was soon apparent that this was not what was going on and my first hypothesis had to be discarded, and replaced by one of quite a different nature. For homework, I asked Eduardo to make a list, either mentally or preferably on a sheet of paper, of past outbursts of anger and circumstances that preceded them.

In our second session, we reviewed Eduardo's mentally prepared list of past incidents that had preceded his outbursts of anger. Together, Eduardo and I learned that Tanya's brief periods of illness seemed to be incidents, which frequently preceded Eduardo's angry tirades, and so did Tanya's anxiety around money and her anxiety around her relationships with her extended family. After talking about these situations for some time, Eduardo and I agreed that Tanya's anxiety around just about anything would trigger his anger.

I proposed to Eduardo that he might get anxious about Tanya's anxiousness and that his anxiety might quickly turn to anger. I reminded him that anger is a secondary emotion and always masks hurt or fear. For some still unknown reason, Eduardo seemed to have trouble handling his wife's anxious feelings. Perhaps, like many men, he felt he should be able to fix things, and felt badly, or even emasculated when he couldn't. In fact, Eduardo's job as a project manager was about fixing things. But Eduardo couldn't fix his wife's illness, or his wife's fears around money, or his wife's anxiety around the problems in her extended family. This explanation seemed to resonate with Eduardo and, for the first time, he looked hopeful about his ability to change. As a man used to problem solving he likely knew that naming a problem was often the first step toward solving a problem. Eduardo agreed to try Thought Field Therapy in an attempt to reduce his anxiety and anger around Tanya's anxiousness.

While Eduardo thought of his wife feeling anxious, he could feel himself getting anxious, upset and angry. We used the Thought Field Therapy anxiety/anger algorithm and Eduardo's soon reported his level of anger and anxiety around his wife's anxiousness at a SUD level of one. Eduardo was challenged to go through several different scenarios in which his wife might feel anxious and consequently he feel anxious and angry. There were two of these scenarios that still had some power to trigger Eduardo's feelings of anxiety and anger. We addressed these two, very different scenarios separately using the same anxiety/anger algorithm. Eduardo was soon able to scan any possible scenarios he could think of without being able to conjure up any feelings of anxiety or anger.

Eduardo came in for his third session looking quite serious. After a short time, he said that there was something he really needed to talk about. He had not experienced any feelings of anxiety or anger around Tanya's anxiety during the past week. However something disturbing had happened; Eduardo had experienced a flashback that woke him up from a deep sleep. The flashback involved an incident he had experienced in Vietnam.

Eduardo, a conscientious objector during the Vietnam conflict, had been assigned as a medic to two tours in Vietnam. On a particular occasion there had been an ambush, and Eduardo had found himself separated from his medical kit. To his right a young soldier lay dying. To his left lay his medical kit. Between himself and his medical kit flowed a steady stream of crossfire. Eduardo crawled through the artillery fire and retrieved his kit. In spite of his valiant efforts, the young soldier whose life he was determined to save lay dead.

For many years following his return from South East Asia, Eduardo had been tortured on a nightly basis by this memory. Over time, this incident intruded with less and less frequency. At the time of our meeting, it had been several years since Eduardo had been awakened from his sleep by this memory. But, as is often the case when doing Thought Field Therapy, underlying problems soon make their presence evident when more superficial ones are successfully addressed.

Following his flashback, Eduardo instantly realized that his problem with anger was intrinsically bound to this long ago tragedy. Eduardo explained that, as a medic, he was trained to keep his medical kit by his side at all times. Because his medical kit was separated from him, he felt responsible for this young soldier's death. In Eduardo's mind this tragic incident had been frozen in time; a young soldier had needed his help, and Eduardo had been helpless to save him.

It was now apparent that after returning from Vietnam when someone close to Eduardo had a problem and he was helpless to fix it, this same fear overwhelmed him. Eduardo agreed to address this long-ago incident in our therapy. However, Eduardo didn't want to talk about the incident in any more detail as he said it was much too painful. Eduardo really didn't want to think about this incident either. He did agreed to think about the incident while doing Thought Field Therapy if there was a chance that it might help him come to terms with this painful memory. I asked Eduardo,"Given the fact that this happened and the fact that there is nothing that you can do about it now, how would you like to feel about the fact that this happened?" Eduardo answered that he would like to feel "at peace."

As he thought about this past trauma, Eduardo could not hold back his tears and he reported a SUD level of ten as we began the Thought Field Therapy trauma/anxiety algorithm. Soon after his SUD level reached four he reported that his SUD level had gone back up to a ten. I asked Eduardo if he was still feeling exactly the same feelings about exactly the same thing. Eduardo was thinking about the same exact thing, only this time he was experiencing overwhelming feelings of guilt and shame. He reported his feelings of guilt and shame were at a SUD level of ten, while his feelings of grief and anxiety remained at a SUD level of four. Eduardo could not separate out these feelings so we began again, this time with the trauma/ anxiety/ shame/ guilt algorithm. Soon Eduardo reported feeling a SUD level of one while thinking about this incident that had happened so long ago.

Not only did Eduardo report being at peace with the incident but he also reported remembering the incident much more clearly than he had ever remembered it in his flashbacks. With this added clarity, unencumbered by terror, anxiety, guilt and shame, Eduardo could see that there would have been nothing he could have done to save this unfortunate soldier, even if his medical kit had been by his side. Eduardo realized that the soldier had been killed on impact, a fact that somehow had not been available to him consciously prior to our intervention.

Eduardo kept his ten required meetings with me and we talked of many things. Throughout the rest of his therapy he reported an absence of anxiety and anger around his wife's anxiety and an ability to remember the past event in Vietnam with peace and acceptance.

Eduardo's story illustrates that Thought Field Therapy can be, and often is, combined with Insight Therapy. Thought Field Therapy can lead to deeper levels of insight and these deeper levels of insight can bring issues to the forefront that can then be addressed using Thought Field Therapy.

Thought Field Therapy can often reveal the hidden nature of a problem. I often think of Thought Field Therapy as a sort of quantum Insight Therapy. With traditional insight-oriented therapies there is, as a general rule, a very gradual move toward discerning these hidden truths. It is true that traditional Insight Therapy is often punctuated by "aha" experiences, but traditional Insight Therapy is, by any account, a long-term therapy experience. Like sub-atomic particles moving in a world where things appear "here" and then "there" without ever having traveled anywhere between "here" and "there," simple Thought Field Therapy interventions sometimes reveal the deeper nature of a problem without ever seeming to have voyaged the distance between one thought and another. Eduardo's story provided a poignant example of the kind of insight that doing Thought Field Therapy can quickly lead to.

This case study also offers one large and one smaller example of "Tooth-Shoe-Lump."

Eduardo's Thought Field Therapy Recipes:

Anxiety/Anger
Eye, arm, collarbone, little finger, collarbone
9-Gamut Treatment
Eye, arm, collarbone, little finger, collarbone

Trauma/Anxiety/Shame/Guilt:
Eye brow, eye, arm, collarbone, under lip, collarbone, index finger, collarbone
9-Gamut Treatment
Eyebrow, eye, arm, collarbone, under lip, collarbone, index finger, collarbone

Using TFT to Uncover the Layers Beneath The Anger

Frank was not a court referral. Frank was an active member of AA and worked hard in his program, yet, in spite of his years of working the twelve-step program, and after years of working with various sponsors, Frank told me that he was always angry. At meetings, he would feel angry when someone simply looked at him. He would feel like they were looking down at him and judging him negatively.

If someone walked into the room, Frank felt like they were looking at him, sizing him up and finding him deficient. Frank felt this way about everyone but he especially felt this way about women. If a woman entered a room when he was present, Frank felt like she was immediately forming a negative opinion of him as a "worthless and defective human being."

Frank very much wanted a woman in his life, but at the same time Frank hated women for finding him (as he perceived it) inadequate and not good enough.

Frank reacted to these supposed slights with anger and resentment. It didn't take much to set Frank off. If Frank thought someone looked at him the wrong way in a grocery line, Frank was likely to tell the person off and stomp out of the store resisting, with all of his being, his impulse to physically assault them.

We began the use of Thought Field Therapy during our first session as Frank lived in his van and his funds were limited. I wanted to make good use of our time in an effort toward helping him address his anger. I began with Frank imagining himself in an AA meeting and imagining that a woman walked in and looked at him. Frank's anxiety and anger immediately rose to a ten as he imagined himself in this familiar situation. Because I suspected that he had experienced a great deal of trauma in his life, I added the trauma spot to Frank's treatment, and in the session Frank's anxiety was decreased to a level of one by doing the trauma/anxiety/anger algorithm. Frank was slightly encouraged but I agreed with him that the real test would be *in vivo*. We both agreed that Frank needed to notice while attending his next meeting how he felt when a woman walked in and look at him.

Frank came to his next session expressing displeasure with the results of our first session. He reported that he had had several occasions where he had gotten really angry during the past week. When Frank had finished reciting the list of situations in which he had gotten angry, I asked him if he had noticed any differences in the situation that we had worked on last week. Specifically, during this past week, had he felt that he was being judged and scrutinized by others, especially women, when they happened to look at him? Frank sat still for some time and then slowly smiled. Actually, he hadn't experienced these same feelings during the meetings he had attended during the past week. Still skeptical that anything so simple could have helped him with his life-long problem, Frank agreed to pay attention to this former cause of anger in his life and notice what was better as well as what was not better. He would let me know how it went when we met again in two weeks.

The next time Frank and I met we worked on a specific anger that arose when he felt like he or someone else had not been treated fairly. During the past week someone had been rude to a clerk at the convenience store where Frank had been purchasing some items. A man had been loud and had treated the clerk in a patronizing manner. Frank felt personally attacked because this had happened in his presence. He reported that his impulse had been to physically attack the obnoxious customer, but he had resisted. However the alternative was that he had stewed for days about the incident and was still angry just talking about what had occurred.

We talked about his tendency to personalize the actions of others. Instead of telling himself that the rude customer had a problem, Frank felt victimized by the man's behavior.

As I questioned Frank about his past, it emerged that his deceased father had been loud and critical. Frank had never received any sign of approval from this man.

Although Frank had done a tour in Vietnam, it seemed obvious to both Frank and I that his anger and his tendency to feel that others' actions were always directed toward him personally were the result of his difficult childhood.

Frank and I devoted the remainder of the session to working on his anxiety and anger around others' loudness and rudeness. It seemed inconceivable to him that anyone could be okay around this.

I explained to Frank the difference between righteous indignation and anger. He could hopefully learn not to take such actions personally while at the same time retaining a sense that it was not okay for people to be rude or unkind. Frank had to learn that he couldn't control the actions of others and that the actions of others spoke more about who they might be than they did about who Frank was or who anyone else was. In truth the thought that the rude behavior might be about the person who was exhibiting the rude behavior and not about the person it was directed to was a new concept for Frank.

We used the trauma/anxiety/anger algorithm as he thought about other people being loud and rude and he soon reported his SUD level to be at a one.

Frank came to his third session slightly more encouraged by his progress. He was noticing the lack of anxiety and anger, which formerly had resulted from his perception that others, especially woman, were judging him and finding him defective. Because of this reduction in anxiety and anger, he was finding it easier to interact with others at his meetings. He was also, finding himself taking the actions of others less personally, even when they were out of line.

Frank still reported being uncomfortable around women he was attracted to although this was no longer because he thought they were judging him. This feeling of discomfort now had more to do with feelings of worthlessness and shame.

We used Thought Field Therapy to address Frank's sense of discomfort around women and after doing the trauma/anxiety/shame algorithm Frank reported a lack of anxiety while imagining being in the presence of a woman that he was attracted to.

We also talked about the fact that, just as men are frequently initially attracted to a woman because of her physical appearance, women are usually more attracted to men who have a steady income, can take care of themselves financially and who are generally "up and running." Frank had expressed a fantasy that he would find an attractive and wealthy woman who wanted to take care of him. I wanted to help Frank come to terms with reality. His fantasy was not only highly unlikely to materialize but it was an unhealthy one. Relationships that are healthy are about two people who can balance, on the one hand, their desire to be connected with others, with, on the other hand, their ability to stand on their own two feet. I reminded Frank that the healthier he got, the healthier would be the people who were attracted to him.

Frank's sessions were spread out over a period of time and we worked on many things. We worked successfully on his great sadness over the loss of his "best friend," a beloved dog that had been Frank's van- mate for years. We worked on Frank's sadness around his father's death and his sadness around the difficult relationship he had had with his father. In Frank's case, these issues of grief did not respond to the use of the simple Thought Field Therapy algorithms and I began using the more advanced diagnostic level of Thought Field Therapy with Frank as we addressed these problems.

After many months of sporadic meetings we eventually began to address Frank's issues of self-esteem. Frank had finally gotten in touch with how the lack of support and nurturing in his childhood had handicapped him in his adulthood. Not only had there been a lack of nurturing and support during his childhood but he had constantly received messages from his father that he was stupid, incompetent and bad. Frank was now experiencing feelings of both sadness and anger. Frank shared that his anger wasn't especially directed at either of his parents. It was simply anger about the way things were and perhaps anger that God would allow a child to experience such difficulty so early in life. The sadness was that his life had been so difficult.

Frank said, "It was like they gave me these cinder blocks that were crumbling and said 'Go build a house' and then blamed me when I couldn't do it. It was like I was trying to get dressed and I'd put my arm in a sleeve and someone would pull off my pant leg and then I'd put on a sock and someone would pull my arm out of the sleeve." Frank concluded, "No wonder I am where I am."

Frank realized that he needed to put the anger and sadness about his unfortunate childhood behind him if he were to conquer his present difficulty with anger. He also realized for the first time that it would be possible for him to get off disability and lead a normal life. Frank was finally feeling more confident about himself and more hopeful about his future.

The simple algorithms were not sufficient to deal with the layer of anger that Frank was now experiencing. Early in our therapy we had used algorithms to peel the outer layers of the onion but the SUD level reported by Frank around this anger issue was reduced only after the use of Thought Field Therapy at the diagnostic level. Frank reported a SUD level of one after using this more exact method of testing for treatment points and their exact sequence.

Frank attended several more sessions. In one session Frank dealt with his anger around some friends not being there for him. (In actuality he was outgrowing many of his old friends and seeing them more clearly as they really were.) By the end of the session, in which we continued treatment using the diagnostic level of Thought Field Therapy, Frank's anger around his experience with his friends was gone, however he left with a feeling of sadness and disappointment. In our following session we addressed the sadness and disappointment, again using Thought Field Therapy at the diagnostic level.

At one point, we got to a place where Frank focused on his fear that if he had something good, even a feeling that was good, someone would take it away. For two weeks, we worked on this deep fear by talking about the problem and using Thought Field Therapy at the diagnostic level. After two sessions of working on this anxiety, Frank called me and asked me if I could see him on a Saturday. He had had a rather disturbing dream the night before and he wanted to talk about the dream before leaving on a trip to visit his sisters in Kansas. I was happy to meet with Frank to discuss his dream. His dream, it turned out, would have been better described as a nightmare.

Frank had dreamed that he was trying to rescue a woman, another man's wife, from a man who was trying to steal her. He tried in vain to save the woman. He asked for help but instead, toward the end of the dream, the would-be helpers joined in with the man who was abducting the woman. The dream ended with the woman lying naked in the street and a crowd of men licking and sucking on her body. Frank expressed that he still felt "beaten down" by the nightmare.

When working with dream material I often ask clients to gestalt their images. In this method, there is a Jungian assumption that everything and everyone in the dream represents some aspect of the dreamer's inner self. The client is asked to act as if they were each of these people (and sometimes objects) in the dream. The therapist plays the part of an interviewer and the person describes the people (and sometimes objects) in the dream in the first person, rather than in the third person, always using "I" rather than "he" or "she" or "it."

I first asked Frank to be the protagonist in the dream. I asked him to be the man who was trying to steal the other man's wife. As I interviewed this "part" of Frank, he described himself in the following way:

S: "Tell me about yourself."

F. "I'm a bully. I get whatever I want to get. I take what is not mine. I'm powerful."

S. "Do you like yourself?"

F: "I don't like myself."

S: "Why?"

F: "Because I don't have that what that person has. I want what they have."

S: "If you're so powerful, why don't you get your own stuff, your own wife?"

F: "They don't want me. I don't know how to get it without stealing."

S: "From whom do you steal?"

F: "From the innocent, those I see as weak, the gentle, the sweet people, the vulnerable. They don't fight back and I want to have what they have."

F: (Continuing and getting out of character and into himself) "I want to be that person, the person I'm stealing from. I want to be sweet, but not vulnerable."

I then asked Frank to be the wife, the woman who was taken hostage.

F: "I'm scared. I like sex, but I'm scared of the way it's being done. I'd much rather have the love and gentleness. I want to be owned by the gentle one, the loving one, not the insane one."

S: "Who is that one; the gentle one that you would like to be owned by?"

F: (beginning to come out of character and into himself, again) "Loved by the sweet Frank, the beautiful gentle Frank, the Frank who's just starting to wake up, you know?"

Next I asked Frank to be the crowd of men who didn't help, who just went along with the woman's abduction and even participated in it.

S: "As the spokesman for this group, tell me about your group."

F: "We were licking her, sucking on her, it wasn't sexual. She was naked and we were getting our sustenance from her, surrounding her. We were following this man. Like listening to the devil."

S: "Why were you as a group going along with this man?"

F: "He was the leader. He was powerful. He was like the devil."

Finally, I asked Frank to be the Rescuer.

S: "Tell me about yourself. How was it for you?"

F: "I was watching. I felt powerless, overpowered, ripped off, stolen from, abused, violated and totally disregarded. Stolen from. Asking for help and not getting the help. No one was responding to my plea for help. All I could do is watch it happen. There was nothing I thought I could do that I didn't do. Do you know what I'm saying?"

I then asked Frank what he made of all this.

F: "I feel like there's a powerful part of me, but I'm in touch with the wrong powerful part, rather than the sweet gentle part. I don't know how to make that part work so that I could live in this world."

Obviously, the possibility of being vulnerable was a very scary thing to Frank. As a child, Frank had been vulnerable and he had had no support, only hurt and criticism.

We talked about how being open did not necessarily mean being vulnerable if one is grown up and can stand on his or her own two feet. Being open isn't so difficult for those who have a secure sense of self. And yes, one does have to be open in order to have a real adult relationship. Frank would have to lose his fear of being vulnerable if he was ever to let love into his life.

Then Frank told me that on two occasions since I had last met with him, he had met different women who seemed attracted to him. And yet he had made no attempt to spend more time with either of these women, or to make small talk, or suggest that they could meet again. "I just want to be with someone," Frank said, "But I just can't seem to make it happen." "I'm tired of being spiritual. I want to live in this life."

Frank had been on a spiritual path and at the same time, he said, that he wanted to live a "normal" life. Somehow, Frank had come to see these two goals as being mutually exclusive. I suggested to Frank that it was as if in his mind he had come to a fork in the road. From that stopping point, the point where he was stuck, he was seeing two different paths, each going a separate direction, and each having a very different final destination. One road led to the path of higher spirituality and enlightenment. The other road led to a more worldly life including the possibility of having a woman in his life. Frank agreed that was a good description of how he saw things.

I suggested that spirituality and life were not mutually exclusive. I reminded him that Mahatma Gandhi was married and that Jesus seemed to love a good party. In fact, I told Frank, "I believe that real spiritual growth happens in relationships rather than in sitting on a mountaintop. In a relationship you learn to compromise, to give, to sacrifice and to make boundaries and you learn how to love yourself." This seemed a shocking concept to Frank who had held spirituality and the world as being mutually exclusive.

I told Frank that I thought a part of him kept him from having relationships because he was scared that someone more worthy might come along and then he would be rejected and alone. Better to reject the relationship from the start than take a chance and get hurt later. I reminded Frank that you must take a chance if you are to love. We worked a short time on Frank's fear of being hurt. It was six weeks until I saw Frank again for what was to be his final session.

Frank now felt at peace with his world and at peace with his past. He no longer felt or looked like an angry person. Frank began shedding old friends that he had allowed to use and abuse him and he began making healthier friends. He had not yet found a life partner but reported liking himself and being much less judgmental of others.

Frank's case provides an example where algorithms were successful for certain problems and not for other problems with the same client. We can guess that as Frank's problems got more complicated, and less specific, the algorithms were no longer effective. Remember, however, that often very complicated problems respond to the carefully planned use of the Thought Field Therapy algorithms, and frequently, even simple problems may require the use of the more precise level of Thought Field Therapy known as Causal Diagnosis. It is not always the complexity of a problem, or the length of time a person has had a problem, or even the severity of a problem that predicts whether or not the problem will respond to the use of the algorithms or will require the use of Causal Diagnosis.

Frank's Thought Field Therapy Recipes

Trauma/Anxiety/Anger
Eyebrow, eye, arm, collarbone, index finger, collarbone
9-Gamut Treatment
Eyebrow, eye, arm, collarbone, index finger, collarbone

Trauma/Anxiety/Shame
Eyebrow, eye, arm, collarbone, under lip, collarbone
9-Gamut Treatment
Eyebrow, eye, arm, collarbone, under lip, collarbone

Grief/Anxiety
Eyebrow, eye, arm, collarbone
9-Gamut Treatment
Eyebrow, eye, arm, collarbone

Footnote

1. Arthur F. Coca (1994) St. Martin's Paperbacks
The Pulse Test

Chapter 5

Changing Negative Self-Assumptions

"It is the theory which decides what we can observe."

Albert Einstein

❖ ❖ ❖ ❖

When our patients suffer from what is often called low self-esteem, negative self-concept, poor self-image, or negative self-assumptions, we usually relegate these beliefs to the area of "core-issues" and think in terms of long-term therapy and resistance to change. And yet, one of the most delightful ways I have found to use Thought Field Therapy to facilitate rapid change has been in the area of negative belief systems having to do with self-image.

If we are to accept that a brief therapy technique such as Thought Field Therapy can help clients change "core-issues" such as low self-esteem, we do, indeed, need to change our theory. We need to find other ways to look at these issues of self-perception, formerly perceived as so deeply ingrained and difficult to treat.

Thought Field Therapy combined with the Ericksonian technique of reframing can help us do just that. Reframing is a therapeutic technique that helps both the therapist and client look at a problem in a different, more positive light. Brief therapy pioneer, Milton Erickson was a master of the reframe, using this technique with great proficiency with clients who came to visit him from around the world. It is a non-pathological approach and I believe this technique is as important to the therapist as it is to the client. If we continue looking at a problem in the same old way we will often get the same old results. In the case of issues of self-esteem this can often mean a long-term course of psychotherapy with a focus on family history and a focus on the exterior "causes" of the problem in an attempt to gain greater insight into the origins of the problem.

Clients themselves are frequently of the opinion that their current problems, including the feelings they hold about themselves, are "deep seated" and difficult to treat. They commonly believe that they will have to suffer to get better, that it will be hard and difficult work and that "There's no such thing as a quick fix."Clients often arrive for their first session believing that therapy will consist of going back into their past and facing difficult childhood issues for long periods of time. They want us to assist them in an effort to get to the "root cause" of their past and current problems, including what they perceive as their issue of low self-esteem. They often guess that they must be suffering from "low self esteem" or they wouldn't be "allowing these things to keep happening to them" and/or they "wouldn't keep finding themselves in the same situations."

One clients reports, "I could never please my mother; nothing was ever good enough. Now I work endlessly to make things perfect. But they are never perfect enough." Another client remembers, "My father told me I was too ugly and too smart and I would be lucky to find a man that would marry me. Now, I settle for anything. I feel no one else would ever want me and that I better settle for what I can get." A woman recalls, "My husband told me I was stupid so many times that I now believe it. I can't find the confidence to even look for a job "

While it would be ludicrous to deny that the past influences both the present and the future, Milton Erickson believed that everyday life commonly hypnotizes people and that it is often our therapeutic task to "unhypnotize" them. According to Ericksonian therapist, Stephan G. Gilligan, it is the job of the therapist to "expand a self-devaluing 'intra-personal trance' to a self-valuing 'intra-personal trance' state."[1] Gilligan goes on to remind us that, "Individuals are not generally aware that the problem states are self-generated."[2]

I believe that we do need to briefly acknowledge the past, but then quickly point out to our clients that they are in control of their own internal attitudes about the past and that only they can change those attitudes. This begins the process of restoring (or forming for the first time) an internal locus of control to the client. This in itself becomes an Ericksonian reframe. The client has a whole new way of looking at a problem. Rather than looking at the problem as something from "out there" ("They did this to me"), the client concentrates on the problem as something presently "in here" ("This is how I reacted and this is what I can change"). Only when the problem is "in here" can the client feel powerful enough to do something about it.

Although different from each other in many important ways, both Thought Field Therapy and Ericksonian hypnotherapy techniques differ from more traditional therapy in several ways. Both are non-insight oriented and both assume not only that a quick fix is possible but that it's expected. Both techniques assume that therapy can be relatively painless, and each of these techniques commonly begins by quickly shifting the focus to both the client (rather than the other) and the present (rather than the past).

In the case of "low self esteem" a second Ericksonian reframe takes place when we assist the client in looking at the self-esteem issue as a specific anxiety, which can be addressed by using Thought Field Therapy. The problem has then been transformed through this reframe from a core-issue to a simple anxiety. This is a huge cognitive leap and one, in my experience, quickly made and experienced by clients. (Therapists may have a little more difficulty.) Clients themselves are all too familiar with the feelings of anxiety that accompany their issues of self-perception.

It usually takes a few minutes or more of talk therapy to name the specific anxiety but when the right one is agreed upon, the entire therapeutic intervention, in my experience, is almost an instant one.

The following case examples illustrate that negative self-assumptions can be treated quickly and effectively using a combination of Thought Field Therapy and Ericksonian reframing.

Feelings of Being "Unsuccessful" and "Not Enough"

Jeff was tall, slender and wore his gray hair in a long ponytail. He was a writer and had some success under his belt. His wife, a medical doctor, was more successful financially than Jeff and Jeff reported feeling like a "total failure." Jeff, ever struggling in his chosen profession, felt that he needed to "make it big" to be okay. He was a success in many ways including having successfully parented and supported several children from a former marriage. At the time of our sessions, Jeff's grown children were all doing well and Jeff enjoyed a great relationship with all four of them. Yet Jeff worried about the legacy he would leave to these children. I reminded Jeff that he was leaving a priceless legacy to his children. Jeff had provided nurturing to his children when they were growing up, and while they had not had an abundance of material wealth, they were adequately provided for. Best of all they enjoyed a good relationship with their father as adults. As I reframed success to Jeff, I wondered aloud why that was not enough?

Jeff replied that his current wife complained that he was unproductive. Jeff felt that he constantly sabotaged his own success because he felt "undeserving" and like he was a "bad person." Jeff reported that his mother had frequently put him down and blamed him for things that were not his fault. His father colluded with his mother by doing nothing. This feeling of being a bad person and an undeserving person was clearly formed during his childhood years.

Jeff and I agreed that if he thought of himself as a bad person and an undeserving person he couldn't be financially successful and at the same time remain congruent with his image of himself. Although Jeff was a psychologically sophisticated adult and had shrewd insight pertaining to this problem, this “core issue” had been formed during his early childhood, a time when thinking is very concrete and not at all abstract. In a child’s view, good things happen when you are good and bad things happen when you are bad.

Some people never really outgrow that more primitive thought pattern on an emotional level. Jeff was psychologically and philosophically astute enough that he had outgrown that early philosophy cognitively, but emotionally it continued to rule his life.

Rather than focus on this issue as two separate self-doubts, I chose to frame it as an anxiety about being a bad, and thus undeserving person. This was a familiar feeling for him and with little trouble he was able to work up an anxiety, accompanied by feelings of shame, with an overall SUD level of ten while thinking about how bad and undeserving he felt. We used the anxiety algorithm combined with the shame algorithm and Jeff soon reported feeling a SUD level of one. However the feelings of anxiety and shame around feeling like a bad and undeserving person were replaced by feelings of deep sadness. Because our session time was up we agreed to address the feelings of sadness during our next session.

During the following session, Jeff revealed that his sadness had to do with time lost because of being stuck in his formerly negative belief system and also sadness and grief around having been given these negative messages during childhood. He felt great sadness for the child he had once been and sadness for what could have been if things had been different and his parents had been more supportive during his formative years.

Jeff and I agreed that his parents had likely both done the best they could, considering the way they had been raised. However, it remained sad that Jeff's couldn't have received more support and nurturing. We used the Thought Field Therapy grief algorithm and Jeff's SUD level around this sadness was reduced from a nine to a one. Jeff now reported a feeling of peace and acceptance around his early years.

Another layer of the negative self-assumption "I'm not deserving" appeared during Jeff's third session. This was a belief around not being good enough. Jeff explained that this anxiety was somewhat different than the anxiety he had had around his former belief "I'm a bad person." It had more of a feeling of needing to be perfect and never being enough. As we spoke this seemed to also have to do with a need to be well known and financially rewarded. Jeff had the talent for potentially high levels of success as a writer. He had received some recognition during his earlier years in New York. I reframed success as engaging in and enjoying the process of creativity and as not being afraid to take the risk. Jeff agreed that would be a helpful way to feel about life, especially given his chosen profession, which financially rewards only the chosen few.

Despite agreeing on a new intellectual definition of success, the fact remained that Jeff had deep emotional pain around feeling like he was not enough and around his need to be perfect. Jeff rated this pain at a level of ten on the SUD scale of one to ten. We did the combined trauma/ (included because of the sadness) anxiety/algorithm and soon Jeff reported a lack of anxiety or sadness (a SUD level of one). Jeff now reported that he was not able to work up any feelings of anxiety or sadness when thinking of his current life situation. While still hoping for worldly success, Jeff no longer defined success in the same way. Even more important, he no longer felt that he was "undeserving" or a "bad person."

Jeff felt like he had accomplished his therapeutic goals and in our next and what was to be our last session, Jeff reported that, although he had no guarantees of worldly success, he felt that he was no longer sabotaging his success with negative self-assumptions about being bad and therefore undeserving. Equally as important, he was not currently limiting his notion of success to being financially rewarded. Jeff reported that he was feeling like he was enough despite the fact that he or his life was not perfect.

Jeff's story illustrates how a self esteem issue can be reframed as a specific anxiety and how, in Ericksonian language, Thought Field Therapy can be used to change a self-devaluing trance into a self-valuing trance This case also demonstrates the fact that there may be several layers to an issue such as self esteem, all of them slight variations on the same general theme.

Jeff's Thought Field Therapy Recipes

Anxiety Accompanied by Shame
Eye, arm, collarbone, lower lip, collarbone
9-Gamut Treatment
Eye, arm, collarbone, lower lip, collarbone

Sadness
Eyebrow, collarbone
9-Gamut Treatment
Eyebrow, collarbone

Anxiety Accompanied by Sadness
Eyebrow, eye, arm, collarbone
9-Gamut Treatment
Eyebrow, eye, arm, collarbone

Feeling Unlovable

Laura, a striking redhead, was smart, attractive, physically fit and unhappy. She initially came asking, "Who am I?" Laura had three school-aged children and a husband she described as "everything any woman would want." Laura described her husband Chuck as "thoughtful, faithful, a good provider and a terrific parent." I wondered what more she could want. But Laura wasn't happy in her marriage. She and Chuck had let the romance go out of their relationship and had busied themselves with work and children. Despite Laura's recent urgings, Chuck hadn't become any more romantic.

Laura acknowledged that she had a high need for attention and affection. Adopted as an infant, she had grown up in a family that was chaotic and her adoptive parents divorced when she was nine. Hard as Laura tried, she never met her adoptive father's high expectations. To cope with the chaos in her family, and in an attempt to please her demanding adoptive father, Laura worked hard and became highly organized. In her current life, this pattern had continued resulting in little time being left for romance, even if Chuck were available. Although Laura was the one complaining, both she and her husband Chuck seemed to be colluding in an effort to keep romance at a minimum.

After listening to Laura talk about her difficulties, her high need for organization (and control) was reframed as a fear of making a mistake and not being perfect. Her fear of not being perfect, we both agreed, was directly related to her childhood belief that she was unlovable. Laura had believed as a child that her father had left the family because she wasn't good enough. "If I could only get it right, if only I were perfect, then I would be lovable" seemed to sum up Laura's current belief.

In a second session, I rhetorically advised Laura that I knew she wasn't perfect, she knew she wasn't perfect, everyone else knew she wasn't perfect and furthermore no one but herself expected that she be perfect because she was human and human beings aren't perfect. She agreed to try Thought Field Therapy as a way to alleviate her anxiety and feelings of guilt around her humanness. I referred to Laura's problem as an anxiety around not being perfect and Laura and I agreed that, on the SUD scale of one to ten, a one would represent a feeling of peace and acceptance around her humanness and the inevitability of her making mistakes. We then used the Thought Field Therapy anxiety algorithm combined with the guilt algorithm to address her self-imposed need to be perfect.

After her treatment with TFT, Laura attempted repeatedly to locate her former feelings of anxiety and her former feelings of guilt around not being perfect but she reported that she "couldn't find them." Instead, of her former feelings of anxiety and guilt, she found only feelings of comfort and acceptance around her humanness. Laura was able to picture scenes of relative chaos and not experience her former feelings of anxiety, upset and guilt because she hadn't managed to maintain perfect control of her world.

In our next session, Laura's deeper and more painful feeling of being unlovable was addressed. No matter what Chuck said or did to try to convince Laura that he loved her it was never enough. So entrenched was her belief that she was unlovable, that Chuck's loving words and actions never seemed convincing. This became a self-fulfilling prophecy and eventually Chuck ceased the compliments and praise. Of course, Laura felt even more convinced (if that were possible) that she was unlovable.

Despite our work during the past week's session, Laura rated her feelings of anxiety around her lovability at a ten on a scale of one to ten. She no longer felt a need to be perfect but she felt not one inch closer to feeling lovable. While Laura focused on her anxiety around being lovable we tapped through the Thought Field Therapy anxiety algorithm. She soon laughed and had no trouble believing that she was lovable. Laura reported amazement that she could feel so differently about herself in such a short period of time.

In her next session, Laura reported that she avoided talking to Chuck about things she was unhappy about because she didn't want to upset him and "make him angry." In talking about this fear, it soon became apparent that Laura's avoidance was not due to anything her husband Chuck had done in the past. In fact, Laura could not remember a single instance where she had brought up anything negative with Chuck aside from asking him to be more romantic. Chuck had, in fact, gone to therapy for a brief time with Laura to work on this problem. Chuck had attempted romantic behaviors (i.e., bringing gifts and cards) for several weeks following their therapy, but the behavior had eventually extinguished itself, perhaps, in part, because it had never seemed quite enough for Laura.

Growing up, Laura had learned the hard way that it was not okay to talk about anything that was wrong. Laura was now transferring her old fear about bringing up anything negative to her current situation, and she and Chuck were both being cheated out of the intimacy that can arise when two people share their unhappiness in an attempt to forge an even stronger and more supportive relationship that works well for both of them. We agreed to directly address her fear that Chuck might get angry if she brought up anything that was negative. We used the Thought Field Therapy anxiety algorithm once again, this time reducing from a SUD level of ten to a SUD level of one, Laura's anxiety around bringing up something with her husband that was potentially negative.

Chuck and Laura were able to work out remaining differences simply by talking things through. Laura reported surprise that it had been so easy for her to bring up "negative issues" with Chuck. She also expressed surprise and relief that Chuck had been so receptive and easy to talk to.

Laura's case history illustrates using Thought Field Therapy to address a relationship problem through addressing an issue of self-esteem and an issue of fear. It also illustrates the value of taking a brief family history in an effort to understand the precise nature of the client's unique self-devaluing trance.

Laura's Thought Field Therapy Recipes

Anxiety Accompanied by Feelings of Guilt
Eye, arm, collarbone, index finger, collarbone
9-Gamut Treatment
Eye, arm, collarbone, index finger, collarbone

Anxiety
Eye, arm, collarbone
9-Gamut Treatment
Eye, arm, collarbone

Addressing Issues of Self-Esteem in Couple Therapy

Connie and Jerry had been married for three years and had met on the Yavapai- Apache Reservation where Jerry had worked as a teacher and Connie had worked as a physical therapist. Connie had a child by a previous marriage and Jerry had accepted this child as his own. They had moved to a community off the reservation to "provide a better environment" for their son.

Now established in their new environment they both complained that they suddenly felt "like strangers." They were both busy with work, saw each other infrequently, and Connie explained that the chemistry had gone out of their marriage. Connie stated that she no longer felt attracted to Jerry.

Jerry came from a traditional Northern European background and his family had not been physically affectionate. Although Connie's family had its share of problems, her family was emotionally close and physically demonstrative.

Connie noted that, after their marriage, she was always the one who had to initiate intimacy. She was now feeling undesirable and rejected and had given up trying to connect on a more intimate level with Jerry. She was finding herself picking fights with Jerry just to get attention.

Jerry agreed to begin initiating intimacy. He hadn't been aware of how dependent he had been on Connie to initiate closeness and how passive he had been in this area. Connie, who tended to be passive in most other areas, agreed to be more straightforward about what she wanted and needed from Jerry. Connie also had a problem with procrastination and this bothered Jerry, who wanted to see Connie pursue her own personal goals.

Growing up it had apparently done little good for Connie to ask for what she needed, as her mother had been quite jealous of her and had not encouraged Connie to be successful. Connie could see that her current situation was different and Connie agreed that it was safe to ask for what she needed and it was safe for her to be a success.

When they came for their second session the following week, the couple reported that things were much better. They were communicating even about things that were difficult.

But Connie said that she was filled with self-doubt. When given some suggestions for what that might specifically mean, Connie resonated with both "unworthy" and "incapable." Connie stated that inside she believed "I can't do it." So, she elaborated, "I put it off and get lazy."

Connie had been physically abused in her prior relationship and to make the situation even worse, her parents were apparently still in the habit of verbalizing their concerns regarding Connie's abilities.

I asked Connie to tune into the thought field around her belief that she was unworthy and incapable (the two did not separate out as separate thoughts for her) and she began sobbing. She reported her SUD level at an eight. Connie's SUD level went from an eight to a four as we did the anxiety/shame algorithm, but it stayed stuck at a four. As we talked some more about what she was feelings she stated that she was now in touch with a feeling of "inadequacy and incompetence."

As Connie focused on these feelings, which seemed to be another layer of her feelings of "inner doubt" she reported that she was now experiencing a SUD level of nine. We began a repetition of the anxiety/ shame algorithm and soon Connie reported a SUD level of one. When asked to think about the former feelings of being "unworthy" and "incapable" Connie also reported a SUD level of one. Connie felt so confident that the couple decided to call me only in the event they needed another appointment. When I called the couple approximately six weeks later to see if I should close their case with their insurance company, they reported that things were going much better. Connie was asking for what she wanted and needed and she was not procrastinating. And there seemed to be a spark in their relationship once again.

This case illustrates how issues of self-esteem can be directly addressed in couples' therapy. Connie's therapy also illustrates the need to be alert to the possibility of the "Tooth Shoe Lump"phenomena, even when working with issues of self-esteem.

Connie's Thought Field Therapy Recipe

Anxiety/Shame
Eye, arm, collarbone, under lip, collarbone
9-Gamut Treatment
Eye, arm, collarbone, under lip, collarbone

Following on the next page is a list of suggestions pertaining to using a reframe followed by a Thought Field Therapy anxiety algorithm to address issues of negative self-assumptions. These suggestions are to be used as a springboard to help you on your way to finding your own unique reframes and your own unique ways to use Thought Field Therapy to address issues of negative self-assumptions.

Footnotes

1. Stephen G. Gilligan 1985, (New York: Brunner/Mazel) Generative Autonomy: Principles for Ericksonian Hypnotherapy. In J.K.Zeig (Ed.) *Ericksonian Hypnotherapy: Vol. I, Structures*, p.197

2. Ibid., p.206

Common Negative Self-Assumptions That Can Be Addressed Using TFT	
The Fear or Anxiety	***A SUD level of 1 Would Mean***
Fear of not being perfect	It's okay if I make mistakes. I'm human like everybody else.
Fear of not being lovable	I'm not perfect, but I'm lovable the way I am.
Fear of not being capable	I am capable of many things.
Fear of not being worthy	I'm a worthwhile descent person.
Fear of not deserving	I deserve whatever good fortune comes my way.
Fear of being inadequate	I'm good at many things
Fear of not being good enough	I'm a good enough person.
Fear of not being enough	I am enough.

Note: The right hand columns are ways to frame what a 1 on the SUD scale would mean. These are not affirmations. I am not aware of any evidence that indicates that affirmations are helpful.

Chapter 6

The Use of Thought Field Therapy in the Treatment of Sexual Problems

"May we all develop the strength to love well."

David Schnarch, Ph.D. *Passionate Marriage*

❖ ❖ ❖ ❖

This chapter contains examples of using Thought Field Therapy to address sexual difficulties. In some cases Thought Field Therapy is combined with more traditional sex therapy. In one case, a Neuro-Linguistic-Programming Technique is used to facilitate the use of Thought Field Therapy. In three of the cases presented, the individual was the focus of treatment. In two cases, the couple relationship was the focus of treatment. I have chosen the following cases based on their ability to provide examples involving a variety of sexual problems and examples of a variety of ways to address these problems using Thought Field Therapy.

At the end of the chapter I have provided a list of ways that you could think about using Thought Field Therapy in the treatment of sexual problems.

Some Background

When my children were small I would read to them a book by Maurice Sendak. It was titled *Where the Wild Things Are*, and was about a boy named Max who had behaved badly and had to go to bed without his supper. A jungle grew where Max's bedroom used to be and Max was joined by monsters with whom he bravely frolicked throughout the night. Before long, Max had tamed the monsters, and in return the monsters had declared Max "King of all the Wild Things."

For many years I specialized in treating adults and children who had been sexually abused. During that time I met many wonderful men and women and children who, like Max, had been visited by monsters during the long nights of their childhoods. Unlike Max, however, their monsters were real, and sometimes they came in the day as well as the night. Often these monsters were relatives or family "friends." Frequently these monsters were mothers and fathers, the very people who are entrusted with the care of children and with whom children should be able to feel most safe.

Unlike Max, these children were not able to tame their monsters, because, when it all began, these children were too small and the monsters too big. And rather than bestowing power upon the children, these monsters took the children's power away.

During those years I led several groups for, and saw individually, survivors of sexual trauma. Through the process of their therapy, I would frequently feel at a loss to help these clients with their current sexual problems. At some point in their therapy their symptomology may have been diminished but sexual problems such as hypoactive sexual desire disorder, vaginismus, sexual addictions, and various unwelcome philias would remain. Troubled by this, I sought help from two accomplished sex therapists, Ellen Cole, Ph.D. and Kathleen Todd, MSW, and in the process of being supervised by these two highly trained and experienced experts I, myself eventually became certified as a Sex Therapist. I am deeply indebted to these skilled therapists and would recommend this type of training to anyone who works with clients who have been sexually abused or who work extensively with a variety of sexual problems.

In my current practice I work with a wide variety of sexual problems including sexual abuse. Ever on the lookout for new and better ways to help clients who are experiencing sexual difficulties, I have found that using Thought Field Therapy has dramatically increased my ability to treat sexual problems rapidly and with lasting results.

Few problems are as difficult for clients (and often therapists) to talk about as sexual problems. These problems often challenge our very sense of who we are. Our sexuality lies at the core of our being and plays a large part in the life-long formation of our sense of self. Thus most individuals and most couples who contact us for help with sexual problems are in a great deal of pain when they come in for their initial session. Most have suffered for several years and many even for several decades before seeking help. Some have sought help unsuccessfully in the past. Commonly, previous attempts to resolve these sexual problems have failed because the long-term therapy these clients pursued became too costly and/or the process become too difficult, too slow and/or too painful.

In the following case studies I describe typical therapy situations involving sexual problems where I have found the use of Thought Field Therapy to be beneficial. When I have enhanced the use of Thought Field Therapy with other brief therapy techniques I will attempt to point out which techniques I am using; however, my emphasis will be on Thought Field Therapy, as that it the brief therapy technique I currently use most in my clinical practice. The examples given below will hopefully inspire you, the clinician, to use Thought Field Therapy creatively and compassionately as you treat sexual problems in your clinical practice.

Hyposexual Sexual Desire Disorder Due To Poor Body Image

Hyposexual Desire Disorder is the most common sexual complaint cross-culturally; yet, it is reported by therapists to be the most difficult sexual problem to treat. Thought Field Therapy, when used creatively and insightfully, can help facilitate change even in this difficult-to-treat arena. Following is a case where I have used TFT to treat low sexual desire due to poor body image.

Few of us have perfect bodies. However, there is a great deal of societal pressure to measure up to current cultural ideals of how we should look. Women, judging by advertising and other media representations, need to be tall, thin, and somewhat, but not too, muscular. Men should be even taller, solidly muscular, tan and athletic looking. But the reality is that human bodies come in all shapes and sizes, all of them potentially lovable. While it is frequently true that diet changes and exercise can potentially lead to a longer, healthier life and a greater sense of well-being, we need to remind our clients that loving their bodies just as they are does not eliminate the possibility of making healthy lifestyle changes.

Paradoxically, accepting and loving themselves as they are enables clients to take the steps they need to change and grow. Anxiety, guilt, anger and shame brought about by self-criticism can be paralyzing. Helping our clients rid themselves of these paralyzing negative emotions allows them to become unstuck. It allows them to enjoy the present and, at the same time, be open to changes in lifestyle that are healthier and have the potential to enhance the qualities of their lives.

Often a negative body image is so disabling that it inhibits the healthy expression of sexuality in a relationship. It is in this context that I have used Thought Field Therapy to help many clients, most, but not all of who have been women, eliminate their anxiety around their appearance. Paula provides a typical example of using Thought Field Therapy to treat Hyposexual Desire Disorder due to negative body image.

Paula, a tall, pretty but somewhat overweight married woman in her late forties, was so concerned about her level of attractiveness that she was no longer having sex with her husband John. Paula had gained weight since her marriage to John and John frequently flashed pictures of Paula in her slimmer days, which he proudly kept in his wallet. During our first session, John pulled out his wallet and showed me a picture of Paula on their honeymoon. The picture was of Paula in a skimpy bathing suit, posing hand on hip. The Atlantic Ocean was in the background. John called my attention to how great Paula had looked and how slim she had been nearly ten years ago.

Paula reported that John frequently made comments about her current weight and reminded her how much more attractive she had looked in her thinner days. It was escaping John that this wasn't helping Paula feel more sexual and it wasn't motivating her to lose weight.

John reported that he still found Paula attractive and desirable, but Paula was receiving a mixed message. Paula felt that because of the weight she had gained, John was no longer attracted to her. I informed John that he needed to stop calling attention to how slim Paula had been, and how great she had looked ten years ago. John agreed that what he had been doing wasn't working and he agreed to stop bringing up the past and to stop trying to control Paula's physical appearance. John had unwisely embraced the tactic of "when what you're doing doesn't work, do more of it." John hadn't realized how hurtful this ritual had become to Paula. When I pointed this out to John, he quickly backed off and began complimenting Paula for things he enjoyed about her in the present.

However, John's old tactic had caused Paula a great deal of anxiety and as part of their couple therapy Paula's anxiety around her body would need to be addressed. Paula could hear the words and was intellectually aware that John desired her, but emotionally she felt otherwise. Her cognitions and emotions weren't in sync and her emotional brain was winning out.

I carefully explained to Paula that using Thought Field Therapy to address this issue would not eliminate reasonable concern about how she looked. However if the intervention were successful, it would eliminate the anxiety (which wasn't helpful) around her physical appearance. On a scale of one to ten, Paula reported being at a SUD level of nine in her upset over her present physical appearance. After doing a brief five-minute TFT intervention involving the TFT algorithm for anxiety with the addition of the treatment spot for shame, Paula reported being a one on the scale of one to ten. She could now think of her body without any feelings of anxiety or shame.

The good results of the brief intervention continued through the remaining course of Paula and John's more traditional couple's therapy. Although Paula still desired to lose weight and engage in a healthier lifestyle, she could now enjoy her own sexuality and enjoy the fact that John found her sexually attractive even if her body was not perfect.

Paula's Thought Field Therapy Recipe

Anxiety/Shame
Eye, under lip, arm, collarbone
9-Gamut Treatment
Eye, under lip, arm, collarbone

Treating Impotency by Treating Anxiety

I have found the simple TFT anxiety algorithm to be helpful in treating male clients who reported problems with impotency stemming from performance anxiety.

Al, in his late sixties, reported a recent history of impotency with his prior partner, Doreen. Al had experienced a disappointing sexual encounter with Doreen several months prior to our first visit. As a result of this experience with impotency, Al became anxious that he would have another erectile failure and this had become, indeed, a self-fulfilling prophecy. Each erectile failure had brought even more anxiety for both Al and Doreen. The relationship deteriorated and Al and Doreen eventually broke up. Al reported that his problem with impotence contributed to the breakup but that several other factors had been involved. He reported that no matter what he had done in an attempt to please Doreen, it had never seemed like enough.

At the time Al came to see me he had just begun to date a woman whom he was quite interested in and he hoped that the relationship would eventually develop in a way that would include sexual intimacy. However, Al was terrified that he might have erectile problems in this new relationship. Careful questioning revealed that Al continued to have nocturnal erections and he frequently had an erection when he woke up in the morning, so a physical problem was ruled out. Al and I agreed that his anxiety certainly wasn't going to make the situation any better and was likely contributing to the problem.

Deciding to try Thought Field Therapy, I carefully set up a treatment goal. A SUD of one would mean that Al would be able to feel relaxed and free of anxiety when anticipating a sexual experience and that he would be able to enjoy sexual closeness whether or not he had an erection.

While doing the Thought Field Therapy anxiety algorithm Al focused on his fear of having a disappointing sexual encounter with his new girlfriend. After completing the

Thought Field Therapy algorithm for anxiety, Al reported that his original anxiety level (a SUD of ten) had been replaced by a feeling of calm and relaxation (a SUD of one) while thinking about the possibility that he might not have an erection during a sexually intimate experience.

Al was unable to work up even a trace of this previously ever-present anxiety. We agreed that being free of anxiety concerning whether or not he had an erection would be a win/win situation. Enjoying the pleasure of sexual closeness as an end in itself, even without having an erection, would be satisfying. If Al did have an erection so much the better.

Al's case took an unusual twist in that I did not see him again for about two years.

When I did see Al again, he was married and it was his wife Christine who made the appointment for couple therapy. Al and Christine each described severe difficulties they were having in the relationship, but these difficulties were of a nonsexual nature. During the course of the first couple session, I asked Al and his new wife routine questions including questions about their sexual life. Both enthusiastically replied that sex was the one part of their marriage that was going well. As I interviewed the couple I delicately asked them some more specific questions including asking if Al ever had problems with impotency. Al replied that a couple of years ago he had had some problems in that area for a short period of time. Not knowing if Al was remembering our session, I asked Al if he had gotten any help for that problem. He replied, "No, It just went away." I wondered if Al was just being discreet and didn't want his new wife to know he had previously been in therapy or if he truly didn't remember his session with me.

The next day Al called me to make an appointment change and also to apologize for not having remembered our former work together. He said that he had truly forgotten all about his previous treatment and indeed hadn't recognized me during our recent session. Despite taking Ginkgo Biloba, Al said his memory was not what it used to be. A few hours after our recent couples' session, it had all came back to him. Al related that he hadn't had erectile difficulties since his Thought Field Therapy session nearly two years before.

Not surprisingly, removing Al's fears around future impotency problems had eliminated the problem itself.

Al's case demonstrates a way to set up a treatment goal (a SUD level of one) in a way that directly addresses a problem that you can do something about. I had no way of knowing whether or not Al would have another erectile failure. What I did know was that Al's anxiety about his sexual performance wasn't helping him. His anxiety was something that we could work with. It would have been limiting to set up the treatment goal to be Al obtaining and maintaining an erection. It is often as important to define the goal, as it is to define the problem. Also, Al's case illustrates the long-term effects of treatment with Thought Field Therapy.

Al's Thought Field Therapy Recipe

Anxiety
Eye, arm, collarbone
9-Gamut Treatment
Eye, arm, collarbone

Vaginismus in an Adult Survivor of Childhood Sexual Abuse: A Case Study Combining TFT with Neuro-Linguistic-Programming

Donna, a woman in her earlie thirties,was longing for a mature sexual relationship. Although Donna wanted to be, as she stated "whole" and enjoy mature sexuality, she had fear, dread and disgust around sex. Donna, who experienced chronic vaginismus, had been in several relationships but they had never been fully sexual and they had never lasted more than a few months. At the age of 32, Donna was technically a virgin.

Donna stated that she had grown inpatient with long-term therapy. She felt desperate and wanted results and wanted them quickly. During our first session, Donna focused on a memory of her brother and his friends sexually forcing themselves on her. She described a feeling of nausea and revulsion as she focused on this violent memory. Donna had difficulty staying focused on this memory because of the intense feelings the memory resurrected. As she focused on the memory, Donna described her SUD level as "twenty" on a scale of one to ten. To help Donna stay focused, and to help make the therapy experience less stressful for Donna, I helped her reduce the intensity of her feelings by drawing on my previous training in Neuro- Linguistic Programming (NLP). We used the NLP technique of making the visual picture of her memory smaller, further away and fuzzy, and turning it into black and white rather than color. Using the past trauma/anxiety/anger Thought Field Therapy algorithm, Donna's SUD level was soon a one while focusing on the memory in black and white, small and fuzzy and far away.

When Donna was asked to make the picture of the memory larger again, and clearer, and closer and turn it back into color, Donna could again work up a SUD level of four when thinking about these past traumatic incidents. We repeated the same algorithm and Donna was soon able to remember this incident without the intense feelings, which had formerly been connected to this traumatic memory.

It is important to note that when using this NLP technique to reduce the intensity of a memory, it may be necessary to repeat the procedure several times. For instance, if you had asked the client to make the picture larger and the SUD level shot back up to a ten, then you might work on reducing the SUD level to a very low number before asking the client to make the memory clearer or in color or closer.

Donna had spent many years in therapy dealing with these childhood issues and had obtained little relief from her suffering. As a result, Donna had extreme difficulty believing that the relief she was experiencing could last over time.

However, in her next session and in later sessions, Donna reported that she was able to remember these episodes with her brother with little emotion. Donna was able to remember her difficult relationship with her brother in a more distant and non-emotional way. She was sorry that these incidents had occurred and did not want to pursue even a distant relationship with her brother at this time in her life. However Donna felt quite removed from these traumatic events from the past, which had previously ruled her life and shaped her relationships.

In Donna's case the abuse had happened over time and had been repeated on numerous occasions. The memory she focused on was likely a generalized memory, a composite memory, representative of the many traumatic encounters of this type that Donna had endured at the hands of her brother and sometimes his friends. In Donna's case one Thought Field Therapy treatment was effective in eliminating Donna's distress around the remembered incident and similar incidences. It is important to note that in many other cases, discrete memories need to be treated with Thought Field Therapy individually, one at a time.

In the next few months Donna and I worked on many other issues such as depression, a need to be perfect, and anger at men in general, but the old childhood memories no longer held her captive. Donna began to have confidence in her own abilities and returned to school. Eventually we focused on Donna's presenting problem, the Vaginismus. I began by doing an Ericksonian type intervention, and reframed Donna's Vaginismus as a protection that her body had developed during her days of abuse. Her brother may have sexually abused her but it would have been very difficult for him to have genitally penetrated her.

I used a Neuro- Linguistic Programming technique of asking Donna to go within and asking her to get in touch with that part of her that had learned to protect her when she was a child. Donna had little difficulty getting in touch with this protective part and she visualized this part of her as a female knight in shining armor. Donna was able to see this part of herself as a young and innocent girl and at the same time a fierce protector. I asked Donna to thank her protective part for the Vaginismus.

With sincerity and respect I joined Donna in this ritual. I thanked the part of Donna that was responsible for the Vaginismus. I thanked that part for protecting Donna when she was a young girl growing up in a pretty crazy household. I asked this protective part if she could find another way to protect Donna in the present and in the future. Together Donna and I were able to remind this protective part that Donna now had skills as an adult that she did not possess as a child. In therapy, she was learning to be assertive, and she was learning the art of developing trust slowly, gradually and appropriately. I guided Donna as she asked her protective part if it would be okay to try some of these new, more adult skills as ways of protecting her in the present and future. There was willingness but some fear. We asked this metaphorical protective part if it would be okay to tap on the fear. Only after getting the go-ahead did we used the anxiety algorithm to help Donna let go of her fear around letting go of the Vaginismus.

Donna was now ready to use more traditional sex therapy approaches for Vaginismus. In past therapies these more traditional approaches such as the use of vaginal dilators had been attempted with zero success. These previous attempts using traditional approaches had ended with Donna feeling more shame, hopelessness and disappointment. However, this time, with little effort, Donna began to experience gradual relaxation during attempts to use similar approaches. Rather than using the more traditional dilators that gradually increase in size, I proposed the idea of vegetable therapy. This method utilizes fresh produce as a substitute for the stainless steel or plastic dilators. It is a less expensive method and adds a touch of light humor to the process of inserting objects of gradually increasing circumference into the Vagina to facilitate relaxation and gradual stretching of the outer third of the Vagina's musculature.

During one particular session we focused on Donna's fear of men. She had been fearful of a certain manager at her workplace. He seemed to be paying special attention to her at work, perhaps because she was clever and bright and quite good at what she did. Perhaps he had other intentions, but Donna saw him only as threatening and terrifying. This man had physical characteristics similar to Donna's father who had been mentally ill and sexually ominous in covert ways. We used the simple anxiety algorithm to address Donna's fear of men in general, represented in the present by this manager. The physiological symptoms of fear around men, which in Donna's case consisted of a feeling of pressure in her head, a feeling of clamminess and a rapid heartbeat, dissipated after this session and Donna began to see men as human beings for the first time in her memory.

When using brief therapy techniques in the treatment of sexual problems rooted in trauma, it is well to remember that, even when the distress around the trauma is alleviated, as in the case study above, sexual issues may remain. It is not that the trauma intervention was unsuccessful but that other layers of the problem such as issues around sex, intimacy or gender still need to be dealt with. There may also be issues of loss, grief and sadness. There may be issues of shame and feelings of guilt. And there are frequently issues of anger. In Donna's case, we met a total of ten times and all of the above issues were dealt with using brief therapy approaches.

Donna's Thought Field Therapy Recipes

Past Trauma/Anxiety
Eyebrow, eye, arm, collarbone
9-Gamut Treatment
Eyebrow, eye, arm collarbone.

Depression
Gamut Spot 50X, collarbone,
9-Gamut Treatment
Gamut Spot 50X, collarbone

Anxiety
Eye, arm, collarbone
9-Gamut Treatment
Eye, arm, collarbone

Anger
Little finger, collarbone
9-Gamut Treatment
Little finger, collarbone

Shame
Under lip, collarbone
9-Gamut Treatment
Under lip, collarbone

Treating Specific Sexual Phobias

Sometimes the focus is on a particular sexual activity. This could be a situation identified by the client as a situation that he/she would like to be able to enjoy in the future but anxiety/fear has kept the client from enjoying or engaging in this sexual activity. The usual protocol would be to have the client imagine him/herself in this situation while doing the anxiety algorithm. When anxiety is alleviated around the visualized sexual situation or activity have the client scan similar situations that he/she would like to feel relaxed about in the future. If there are any remaining areas of discomfort these situations can then be addressed using Thought Field Therapy. Remember that these need to be activities that the client has a desire to be comfortable with rather than an activity that they think they should be comfortable with or that their partner wants them to be comfortable with.

Ellen was uncomfortable with oral sex. Her aversion did not seem to be rooted in any trauma, but perhaps had something to do with her rather restricted upbringing. In any case, Ellen wanted to be able to enjoy this sexual activity with her partner. In our first session, I had Ellen visualize herself in a sexual scenario that she would like to be able to experience and enjoy, a scenario that now created anxious feelings. I then had Ellen repeat the TFT anxiety algorithm as she pictured several different anxiety-provoking scenarios. By the end of the first session Ellen could picture herself experiencing and giving oral sex without any feelings of anxiety or discomfort.

Of course, a cure is not a cure until it is maintained over time and while confronting the situation that has been addressed. A week later Ellen called to cancel her second session. Ellen reported that she now felt relaxed about oral sex and if she had any further problems she would certainly give me a call.

Sometimes the treatment for a specific sexual phobia generalizes and the client can then visualize feeling more comfort in the many sexual situations in which she/he previously was not comfortable. However, it is often the case that several of these sexual situations will have to be addressed separately using Thought Field Therapy. Either way, Thought Field Therapy provides a wonderful new tool to use in treatment with men and women who have been sexually abused or who, for other reasons have suffered anxieties and fears around sexual situations.

Ellen's TFT Recipe

Anxiety
Eye, arm, collarbone
9-Gamut Treatment
Eye, arm, collarbone

Of course, most treatments involve more than one session. In our next case discussion, Bill and Nancy's therapy provides an example of the use of Thought Field Therapy within the context of more traditional marriage and family therapy.

Complex Marital and Sexual Issues: Combining Thought Field Therapy with Traditional Sex Therapy and Traditional Couples Therapy

Bill and Nancy had been married for six years and had not had sexual intercourse for the past three. They explained to me that they were each experiencing such severe emotional pain that they would either reach their goal of becoming sexually intimate or they would divorce, and continue on with their lives separately. Nancy felt that Bill had lost interest in her.

She felt rejected by him and suspected and feared that he had lost interest due to the fact that she had gained weight.

After their initial interview, I met with Nancy and Bill individually one time each to take their sexual histories in the tradition of my training in classic Masters and Johnson-style sex therapy.

In Bill's individual session, he reported that he had once been physically attracted to Nancy. In spite of the fact that Nancy was quite large, Bill, who was an artist, reported that he had always been attracted to Nancy's curves. The reason Bill gave for distancing himself from Nancy had nothing to do with Nancy's body. Bill perceived Nancy as controlling and he reported that Nancy frequently demeaned him. Nancy had frequently been critical of Bill's sexual performance and Bill felt intimidated by her. He felt that Nancy put the responsibility for their sexual difficulties solely on him and he needed her to acknowledge that she, too, was part of the problem. Additionally, Bill felt that Nancy did not allow him any space for his feelings and opinions.

In doing a brief family of origin history, Bill reported that his mother had been chronically ill. He described his mother as someone who controlled by using her illness. Due to his mother's neediness and dependence on him, there had been no room in his childhood for his feelings.

Bill stated that he very much wanted his relationship with Nancy to include sexual intimacy, but Nancy, he said, was difficult to please and he never felt adequate. To make matters worse, Nancy frequently compared Bill to past lovers.

Despite his willingness to address the issue of sexual intimacy, Bill expressed a great feeling of relief when he learned that their therapy would initially begin with a no-sex contract, as he and Nancy began the traditional Master's and Johnson Sensate Focus, or touching exercises.

> In the first Sensate Focus exercise, partners meet at an agreed upon time. In most cases they wear no clothing. One partner, (the toucher), explores the other partner's (the touchee's) body with the goal of experiencing how it feels to touch as opposed to the goal of pleasuring the partner. This begins as a non-sexual exercise with breasts and genitals off limits. The toucher touches for as long as he or she wants (unless the touchee is uncomfortable). When the toucher is finished, the partners switch places and the toucher becomes the touchee and the partner begins the experience of "touching for his or her own pleasure."

Toward the end of our therapy session, Bill mentioned that he reacted with intense anxiety when Nancy expressed any disappointment in him. Bill stated that he reacted to Nancy's frequent expressions of disappointment by emotionally and physically withdrawing. Eventually Bill's anxiety would build to a point where he would experience anger and resentment and rather, than acting out, he would react by retreating even further within. This resulted in Bill being distant and emotionally unavailable. I suggested that we try using Thought Field Therapy with the thought that reducing Bill's anxiety around Nancy's expressions of disappointment might help him stay more present to work on the relationship. In our session, Bill had no problem working up an anxiety with a SUD of about nine just thinking about the possibility of Nancy expressing disappointment in him. Using the simple Thought Field Therapy anxiety algorithm, Bill soon reported an absence of anxiety or fear when thinking about Nancy expressing disappointment.

The next day I saw Nancy for her individual appointment. Nancy stated that her marriage had felt like six years of continual rejection. She added that sex with Bill, from her perspective, had never been satisfying. She emphasized her point by relating that she experienced anxiety and feelings of rejection whenever she was in their bedroom.

Nancy agreed to try Thought Field Therapy in an attempt to reduce her current anxiety around her relationship with Bill as represented by that room. She reported a SUD level of eight when just thinking about their bedroom. We used the Thought Field Therapy algorithm for trauma/anxiety and Nancy's anxiety around their shared bedroom and the feelings of rejection that their bedroom had come to symbolize for her were reduced to a one. She was no longer personalizing the current lack of sex in the relationship and the bedroom was, once again, at least a neutral zone.

During this session, Nancy also reported that her relationship with her parents had been, and still was, extremely difficult. Her mother was ineffectual and not there for her. She experienced the most disappointment, however, in her relationship with her father. Nancy lamented that her father could never "get who I am."

As Nancy began to relate specific incidences having to do with her relationship with her father, his personality traits emerged, such as his need to be right, his constant criticism of her and his rage when anyone dared to infer that he was less than perfect. I shared with Nancy that her father was likely a Narcissistic Personality disordered person or at least a person who was severely narcissistically impaired. Unfortunately for her, he was quite unlikely to change.

I explained to Nancy that this was about her father's limitations and not about her, but Nancy did not experience my statement as good news. Just thinking about her painful relationship with her father combined with my prediction that he was unlikely to change brought tears to her eyes. Nancy was soon sobbing uncontrollably and when asked, reported a distress level of ten. We did the Thought Field Therapy grief algorithm and soon Nancy reported peace and acceptance (a SUD of one) around the fact that her father would likely never be who she wanted and thought she needed him to be.

A week later I met with both Nancy and Bill. Bill reported that he was no longer reacting with anxiety, which in the past had quickly turned to anger and distancing, when Nancy expressed disappointment in him. Nancy acknowledged that Bill had been more present in the relationship since his individual session. Nancy happily reported that she had been comfortable during the two conversations she had with her father during the previous week and she had not been triggered by his lack of "getting who I am."

While Nancy was initially experiencing a great deal of difficulty with and resistance to the no-sex contract, Bill was enjoying the non-sexual touching for his own pleasure (the first part of the prescribed exercises). Bill was used to doing things for others and the concept of touching for his own pleasure had never before occurred to him. When she understood that the exercises could be helpful to their ultimate goal of being sexual, Nancy reluctantly agreed to continue with them. I proceeded to give Nancy and Bill their second Sensate Focus Exercise and we agreed to meet the following week.

> The second Sensate-Focus exercise is precisely like the first, except that this time, touching breasts and genitals is allowed. The couple is reminded that this continues to be a non-sexual exercise. It continues to be touching for "your own pleasure" and the touching is not to be thought of as foreplay or as an attempt to pleasure the partner.

At the beginning of their next session Nancy and Bill excitedly reported a major insight they had immediately following their most recent sensate focus exercise. They related the following story:

Shortly before they were married Bill had shared with Nancy a commitment he had made to himself earlier in his life. Bill had felt a need for a spiritual retreat and had decided to spend some time in solitude in the desert. He had been trying to find the time to make this retreat for several years. Fearing that the constraints of marriage would make this journey even more difficult to undertake, Bill asked Nancy for her blessings and asked to take his retreat before their marriage.

Nancy replied, "If you go, don't expect me to be here when you get back!"

Bill was torn. He wanted to marry Nancy but also wanted to take this longed-for respite. He decided against making the retreat and Bill and Nancy soon married. Bill ended up going through with the wedding with mixed feelings. Bill and Nancy reported that even the wedding pictures revealed Bill's unhappiness. Bill stated in this session that he had felt that Nancy would always have things her way and that his needs and his feelings would never be important. Bill admitted that he still to this present day harbored resentment about this incident.

Resentments over events from the past frequently linger and cause unspeakable pain and damage to an otherwise good relationship. Such a situation is an excellent opportunity to use Thought Field Therapy to heal these resentments, hurts and angers. In Bill and Nancy's case, Bill agreed that he would like to put this episode behind him. With Nancy present in the session, Bill was able to work up an anger level of seven just thinking about this emotionally laden experience. Using the TFT simple trauma algorithm combined with the anger algorithm, Bill was able to alleviate his feelings of anger around this memory. With his anger out of the way, he was able to empathize with Nancy's past feelings of fear of abandonment. Most important, it now felt to Bill like something that had occurred in the past, which no longer had any bearing on the present. Thanks to Bill and Nancy's insight we were able to use Thought Field Therapy to remove this enormous obstacle from their path to a closer and more intimate relationship.

By the seventh session, Nancy and Bill reported that they had recently begun having sexual intercourse (a little ahead of their sensate focus exercise schedule). However, Nancy, still difficult to please, complained that her orgasms weren't always as powerful and dramatic as she would like them to be. With a little help, Nancy was able to see that in her dissatisfaction with anything less than perfect she was a little like her father. If things weren't perfect she was disappointed. Uncomfortable as the analogy to her father was, she let the comparison sink in and this became an "Aha" experience for Nancy. With a little probing, Nancy acknowledged that she felt anxiety when things were not perfect. In this session, she was able to tune into her anxiety around lack of perfection and using the Thought Field Therapy anxiety algorithm her anxiety around a lack of perfection in her life and in the world was reduced to a one.

Bill and Nancy moved to another area not long after their last session. When they were settled they gave me a call and let me know that they were enjoying each other as sexual partners and as friends. In Nancy's words, "Things are much better, at least most of the time. Everything's not perfect, but that's okay."

In just seven sessions, Thought Field Therapy combined with more traditional sex therapy helped this couple successfully resolve core issues that had been interfering with their desire to have a satisfying, intimate and sexual relationship.

This case history illustrates how Thought Field Therapy can be used with traditional sex therapy approaches such as the Masters and Johnson Sensate Focus Exercises. (For a more complete and detailed description of Masters and

Johnson Sensate Focus Exercises please see: *The Illustrated Manual of Sex Therapy* (second edition) by Helen Singer Kaplan, M.D., Ph.D.)

Bill and Nancy's Thought Field Therapy Recipes

Bill's Anxiety:
Eye, arm, collarbone
9-Gamut Treatment
Eye, arm, collarbone

Nancy's Grief:
Eyebrow, collarbone
9-Gamut Treatment
Eyebrow, collarbone

Bill's Trauma/Anger:
Eyebrow, collarbone, little finger, collarbone
9-Gamut Treatment
Eyebrow, collarbone, little finger, collarbone

Nancy's Anxiety:
Eye, arm, collarbone
9-Gamut Treatment
Eye, arm, collarbone

The following list may serve to remind you of some of the opportunities you might encounter where the use of Thought Field Therapy could make addressing sexual issues even more efficient and effective. This list will be of most benefit to the therapist who has taken, at minimum, the Callahan approved Thought Field Therapy algorithm training.

Examples of Sexual Issues that May Be Addressed Using Thought Field Therapy

1. Hypoactive Sexual Desire Disorder (Lack of Sexual Desire)

A. When lack of desire has to do with anxiety about appearance.

B. When lack of desire has to do with anxiety about performance.

C. When lack of desire has to do with past trauma.

D. When lack of desire has to do with anger.

E. When lack of desire has to do with guilt.

F. When lack of desire has to do with shame.

G.. When lack of desire has to do with embarrassment.

2. Male Erectile Disorder (Impotence)

A. Anxiety due to a disappointing sexual experience in the past.

B. When Erectile Disorder has to do with anger.

C. When Erectile Disorder has to do with guilt.

D. When Erectile Disorder has to do with shame.

E. When Erectile Disorder has to do with past trauma.

F. When Erectile Disorder has to do with embarrassment.

3. Vaginismus

A. When Vaginismus is due to past trauma.
B. When Vaginismus is due to anxiety (about appearance/about performance).
C. When Vaginismus is due to guilt.
D. When Vaginismus is due to shame.
E. When Vaginismus has to do with embarrassment.

4. Premature Ejaculation

A. To reduce anxiety around the problem. (This is especially true for the male partner experiencing the problem, but anxiety reduction can be helpful to the partner as well.)
B. To reduce anger in either the person experiencing the problem or the partner.
C. To reduce shame around the problem.
D. To reduce guilt around the problem.

5. Addictive Sexual Behaviors

As with other addictive urges, these addictions have become ways the client has learned to cope with anxiety. Treating anxieties, past trauma, anger, guilt, shame and embarrassment can be an important part of effective long-term treatment of sexual addictions such as Sexual Sadism, Frotteurism, Exhibitionism, Pedophilia, Voyeurism, Sexual Masochism and undesired sexual activities such as cross dressing.

6. Gender Identity Disorder

Thought Field Therapy techniques can play a part in the treatment of Gender Identity Disorder. Treatment goals appropriate for short-term therapy include:

A. Comfort with one's own body regardless of gender and/or sexual orientation.
B. Comfort with activities that are feminine or masculine.

Chapter 7

Using Thought Field Therapy with Cognitive Therapy

"The greatest discovery of my generation is that a human being can alter his life by altering his attitudes of mind."

William James

❖ ❖ ❖ ❖

Cognitive Therapy was once the "crazy new therapy of the '50s." Since its inception, it has weathered the storms that revolutionary ideas create and emerged to become one of the most respected psychotherapy modalities today. While Cognitive Therapy has some notable limitations, Cognitive Therapy can be useful at times in setting up a problem in such a way that it can be successfully treated using Thought Field Therapy.

For instance, clients sometimes believe that another person's actions "caused" them to behave in a certain way. Frequently clients make comments such as, "If she hadn't provoked me by calling me a loser, I wouldn't have hit her," or "If she hadn't put me down in front of the other people at work, I wouldn't have gotten so upset," or "If my daughter would have come home at a reasonable hour, I wouldn't have lost my temper and called her those names."

The pioneer of Cognitive Therapy, Albert Ellis reminded us that the event does not cause our reaction. If the event caused our reaction, everyone in the world would react in the same way to the same event. There is something that happens between the event, and our reaction. Albert Ellis called this "Self-Talk." It is what we say to ourselves about the event that causes our own unique response. As adults and short of torture, no one has the power to make us behave in a certain way. Cognitive Therapy helps clients begin to think about their need to change their reactions to certain events that take place in their lives.

Ellis actually called his new therapy Rational Therapy and Aaron Beck renamed it, Cognitive Therapy. However, whether we know it as Rational Therapy or Cognitive Therapy, this technique can help clients discover their dysfunctional beliefs and their troublesome self-talk. Once these problematic beliefs and troublesome self-dialogues are identified, a therapist can begin the process of using Thought Field Therapy to assist clients in their effort to replace old beliefs with new ones and old ways of talking to themselves with new ways of talking to themselves.

Some popular dysfunctional beliefs are: "I have to be loved by everybody all the time," "It's awful when things don't go the way I want them to go," "I have to be perfect and competent in everything I do and say," "I need to be in control at all times or something bad might happen," "If someone is angry with me, I must have done something wrong," "The world is a scary place," "People can't be trusted," "People will always let you down," "If you want something done right, you have to do it yourself," and, the ever popular, "Other people should behave the way I think they should behave," or "Things should always go the way I think they should go."

Dysfunctional self-talk usually reflects one or more of the above beliefs or one or more similar beliefs.

Years ago I would have asked a client who was addressing a specific issue such as anger or anxiety to keep a self-talk journal. I would ask them to note the event that triggered their unwanted emotion and then write down their reaction to that event, and the repercussions of those reactions. Then I would ask them to attempt to identify their self-talk, what they had said to themselves to cause their reaction. Next the client would write down what they might have said differently to themselves to increase the likelihood of a different, more desirable reaction and what the repercussions of that more desirable reaction might have been.

Using this cognitive-behavioral approach, clients would eventually learn new ways of looking at the world and new ways of talking to themselves. That is, if they stuck with their therapy long enough and if their problems were not connected to a significant trauma.

How Cognitive Therapy Can Be Helpful in Using TFT

Identifying a client's dysfunctional belief or beliefs can help set up a client's problem so that it can be addressed with Thought Field Therapy succinctly and effectively in a short period of time. A client may present, for instance, with the primary complaint of procrastination. While talking about this you might find that the client puts off things because if she did them she would have to do them perfectly. This internally generated demand for perfection creates so much anxiety that, as a result, almost nothing gets done. "Better not to do it than to risk not doing it right" is this client's unconscious conviction.

This client might have a disabling belief that everything she does needs to be perfect. She may fear not being perfect and/or she may fear making a mistake. Her dysfunctional belief might be, "I need to be perfect in everything I do." Or it could be "It's a terrible thing if I make a mistake." Both of these dysfunctional beliefs are related to that old familiar saw, "Anything worth doing, is worth doing right." Although these two beliefs are similar, one statement may resonate more with one client and the other with another client. It is best to go with the statement that resonates most with the client.

In our hypothetical case, the goal (a SUD level of one) could be set up as an absence of anxiety around doing something that's not done perfectly, or an absence of upset around making a mistake, or not being perfect in some other way. The resulting change in cognition would then be something like, "It's okay if everything isn't done just perfectly," or "It's okay if I make a mistake. I'm human, so I can't be perfect."

I want to emphasize that Cognitive Therapy approaches are most helpful in the first stage of treatment: identifying and refining the problem. Once therapist and client have identified the precise belief, the Thought Field Therapy anxiety algorithm can, in most cases, then be used to address the identified problem quickly and effectively. It has been my observation, that clients' cognitions change almost instantly when Thought Field Therapy has been successfully used to treat a problem. This is true whether or not Cognitive Therapy was formally used as a part of setting up the problem.

A Need to Be in Control

Probably the most common dysfunctional belief is the one that goes something like: "I must be in control of everything and everyone at all times "

With many people anxiety can be extremely intense when they feel they are not in control. They may get more upset than the rest of us when their children disobey or get in some kind of minor trouble at school. An undone homework assignment, a child staying out even slightly after curfew, or a small untruth told by a teenager who wants to go somewhere he is normally not allowed to go can seem like a life threatening crisis to a person who suffers this particular form of anxiety. Similarly, a husband who comes home an hour late from work, or a wife who doesn't cook the potatoes just the way he likes them to be cooked, or a forgotten Valentine's card can seem like out-of-control disasters to those who feel a strong need to be in control.

The following story illustrates how needing to be in control can manifest in anxiety and strain a relationship to the breaking point. It also illustrates the importance of identifying faulty cognitions and dysfunctional beliefs.

Glenda had been married eighteen years to a successful building contractor. They had a fine home and four children. Glenda and her husband were active in the community, popular socially, and unhappy in their relationship. Glenda came in initially for individual therapy. Her husband was so unhappy with her that he was contemplating divorcing her if she didn't get help.

In the beginning Glenda failed to see any legitimacy in her husband's complaints about her. She dismissed them as petty and was in fact unclear what his problem with her really was. However, Glenda did complain that her husband Morey didn't take her seriously. She described Morey as a *"bon vivant"* who was more interested in making money and leading the good life than he was in her as a person or in his family. From her perspective, Morey was difficult to please and went out of his way to find fault with her.

During our first session, I learned that Glenda's parents divorced when Glenda was a teenager. The divorce took Glenda and her two siblings by surprise. Glenda had been close to both her father and her mother and Glenda, as of our first meeting, had not made peace with this early disappointment in her life. As Glenda shed tears of sadness around what she saw as the disintegration of her family as she had known it, we did some grief work around this early loss and the devastation it still seemed to create in Glenda's present life. Using the Thought Field Therapy grief/anxiety algorithm, Glenda soon reported feeling peace and acceptance around this childhood trauma.

Glenda came to her second session feeling much more resolved around the issue of her parent's divorce. However, Glenda continued to feel unsettled and anxious about her relationship with her husband. Glenda didn't want a divorce and wanted to keep her family together. The potential of a marital breakup was quite unthinkable to Glenda. She was adamant about not wanting to put her children through what she had gone through.

Glenda, in an attempt to explain what was wrong with her relationship, began by reconstructing incidents from the past designed to let me know what was "wrong" with Morey. I explained to Glenda that we could be in therapy for years if we continued to dwell on incidents from the past. I explained that couple therapy is about attempting to create a better present and a better future. With a little coaching Glenda was able to look forward and describe what she did want from her husband. She wanted Morey to be more involved with the children in the not–so–fun things, like disciplining and picking up after them. Currently, Glenda felt that she was always set up by Morey to be "the bad guy." Morey's interactions with the children consisted of defending them against Glenda and having fun with them.

Even more important to Glenda was that she wanted to be able to bring up issues such as co-parenting the children in a conversation, even if it was perceived by Morey to be "negative" and/or unpleasant. Glenda didn't feel like Morey ever really listened unless it was something he wanted to hear.

It was becoming increasingly clear that if our goal were to preserve this marriage, Morey would need to begin attending these sessions. I was still unclear as to what Morey's complaints were and what was making it so difficult for him to remain in this relationship. I had already met individually with Glenda two times, so I elected to invite Morey to come in for an individual session before exploring the possibility of moving into conjoint therapy. I needed to know if Morey wanted to work on his marriage, and I needed to be clearer about what Morey's needs were.

In his individual session, Morey stated that he was "worn out." He felt that "everything was going out and nothing was coming back in." Morey reported loving his job and that life, in general, was good. However he experienced home as "another story." Morey complained that Glenda was "always down." At home, Glenda was always yelling at the children. Morey saw Glenda as a person who would inevitably find something wrong. Even in public, when out with friends, Glenda would make negative remarks about Morey, and he reported that friends were noticing this and commenting on Glenda's behavior.

I asked for examples—not to dwell on the past, but in order to determine if there was a common thread that wove through Morey's complaints. As Morey related one example after another it became increasingly clear that the common thread was that Glenda just couldn't roll with the unexpected. Glenda, a highly organized individual, needed things to go smoothly. However, life usually doesn't go smoothly. Things do go wrong. But, for Glenda, when something didn't go exactly as it "should, " she "snapped." Frequently this escalated to the point where Glenda was yelling. Morey stated that he had tried everything he could and he commented, "It's just the way she is." Morey went on to say that he just couldn't take it anymore and he needed out.

I optimistically suggested that Glenda could change. Morey expressed great doubt. I told him that, from my perspective, Glenda quite simply suffered from an anxiety about not being in control. When things didn't go exactly as planned, it was very frightening to Glenda. I told Morey that these anxieties are usually quite easy to fix. Morey stared at me in disbelief. It was if I were trying to sell him the Brooklyn Bridge. Reluctantly, Morey agreed to give couple therapy a try.

During our first conjoint session, we focused on what Morey could do to make things better for Glenda. Morey agreed to listen to Glenda, even if the content of what she had to say was negative, provided, he added, "That she is not yelling at me while she is sharing this information." Morey agreed to do only active listening unless Glenda specifically asked for advice or feedback. (Like many men, Morey saw his job as needing to fix problems not listen to them.) Glenda, for her part, agreed to be pleasant. They would, at the end of the day, share what they liked about each other. If Glenda found it difficult to be pleasant even when things were not going according to plan, we would address this issue during our next session.

The following week Glenda and Morey reported that things were much improved. They agreed that focusing on what they liked about each other had been most helpful. Both had enjoyed the evening exercise of focusing on what they found positive about the other person.

Morey had realized that he had been bringing his take-charge business persona home and he was now leaving it at work where it belonged, changing hats before he entered the front door of their home. And, he was actively listening to Glenda. Now that Glenda felt listened to there was a way for the couple to talk about some of their difficulties such as sharing the responsibility of raising the children. They had had two small arguments and Glenda, with a little help, became aware that these incidents had both evolved from her feelings of being out of control. Glenda acknowledged that she believed that she needed to be in control at all times or something bad would happen. We agreed that this likely stemmed from her childhood experience of feeling so out of control when her parent's divorced.

Glenda knew, rationally, that no one can be in control at all times, however, she acknowledged that she had a dysfunctional belief that told her that she should always be in control. When things were not perfect, it was scary for Glenda. It signaled to her that she was not in control. I reminded Glenda that ultimately no one is in complete control. She would need to make peace around this. I asked Glenda to focus on her anxiety around not being in control of everything. She reported a SUD level of seven. We used the Thought Field Therapy grief/anxiety/anger/algorithm and in a few minutes, Glenda was reporting a lack of anxiousness around the fact that she could not always be in control. Glenda said it this way: "I know that I can't be in control all the time and that's okay." In this session, Glenda was able to shift her cognitions and her self-talk around needing to be in control.

Our fifth session was also our last session. Glenda and Morey agreed that they were doing much better. Morey no longer had thoughts of leaving the marriage. Glenda reported an absence of her old knee-jerk reaction when something didn't go perfectly. Just as important, Glenda felt like Morey was really listening. Glenda agreed to call me if she experienced any reoccurrence of her old anxiety.

Glenda's Thought Field Therapy Recipes

Grief/Anxiety/Anger
Eyebrow, eye, arm, collarbone, little finger, collarbone
9-Gamut Treatment
Eyebrow, eye, arm, collarbone, little finger, collarbone

Anxiety
Eye, arm, collarbone
9-Gamut Treatment
Eye, arm, collarbone

Following is a list of dysfunctional beliefs that can be addressed using Thought Field Therapy. This is not a comprehensive list but it presents examples of ways that dysfunctional beliefs can be identified during the first phase—setting up the problem.

The following list also gives examples of ways to frame corresponding beliefs, which would be more functional and would be represented by a SUD of one.

Common Dysfunctional Beliefs That Can Be Addressed Using Thought Field Therapy

The Dysfunctional Belief	A "1" on the SUD Scale Would Mean
I must be in control of everything at all times.	I can't control others or the world and I have peace around this.
It's not okay to have my own needs.	My needs are important too.
I can't say the truth if it hurts someone.	Sometimes others need to hear the truth and sometimes I need to say what's true even if it's difficult.
If someone is angry with me, it's my fault.	Sometimes anger is about them and not about me.
It's not okay to be angry.	Sometimes it's okay to be angry.
Love should be perfect.	People are imperfect, so love can seem imperfect.
I am entitled to a life that is pain-free.	Life doesn't have guarantees and I accept that.
I need to be loved by everybody all the time.	It's okay if someone doesn't like or love me.
I need to be perfect in everything I say and do.	It's okay if I'm not perfect.
People should behave or think the way I think they should.	I can't control the way others think or behave and that's okay.

The Dysfunctional Belief	A "1" on the SUD Scale Would Mean
Life is supposed to be fair.	Life doesn't seem to be fair and that's okay.
It's not okay to make a mistake.	I can make a mistake and it's okay.
Conflict is bad and I need to avoid it at all costs.	Conflict is a necessary part of life and I can accept and face this with comfort.
Other people's needs are always more important than mine.	My needs are important too. It's okay to love myself.

Chapter 8

When Cognitive Therapy Doesn't Help: Using Thought Field Therapy to Treat Trauma

"Because people are most aware of the verbal, rational part of their brains, they assume that every part of their mind should be amendable to the pressure of argument and will. Not so. Words, good ideas, and logic mean nothing to at least two brains of three. Much of one's mind does not take orders."

Thomas Lewis, M.D., Fari Amini, M.D.,
Richard Lannon,M.D.
A General Theory of Love

❖ ❖ ❖ ❖

While Cognitive Therapy can sometimes be helpful in the treatment of non-trauma related psychological problems, it took neuroscientist Joseph Le Doux to help us understand why Cognitive Therapy is of limited effectiveness when dealing with trauma. With careful research, Le Deoux demonstrated that traumatic memories are stored in a way that is quite different from the way other memories are stored.[1]

Previous to Le Doux's research, it was believed that information of a possibly life-threatening sort would enter the brain in much the same way as more normal everyday, less emotionally laden information. That is, the information would enter the brain through the sensory organs (the eyes, the nose, the ears, the mouth, the skin) and the information would be then directed to the thalamus where it would be sorted out and sent to the appropriate area of the cerebral cortex. Information that entered through the eyes would be directed from the thalamus to the visual cortex; information that entered through the ears would be directed by the thalamus to the audio cortex; etc. Then, something very different from the way more normal information is stored would occur. Emotionally charged information containing, possibly life-threatening data would be sent from the cerebral cortex to the amygdala, a part of the limbic system that is responsible for giving emotional charge to an environmental situation.

But Le Doux and his colleagues discovered that traumatic, emotionally charged information is sent to the amygdala in quite a different way. Instead of traveling from the thalamus to the appropriate area of the cerebral cortex, trauma related information is launched via a separate pathway directly to the amygdala itself. This explains the limitations of Cognitive Therapy relative to severe emotional trauma.

Cognitive Therapy is dependent on our ability to reason. Our ability to reason involves our ability to employ our cerebral cortex. The emotions related to traumatic events seem to have minimal connection to the cerebral cortex. Joseph Le Doux demonstrated this in a now well-known experiment. Le Doux destroyed the audio cortexes in the brains of a group of laboratory rats. He then simultaneously exposed these rats to the sound of a bell and an electric shock.

After a series of repetitions, each exposing the rats to the sound of the bell and the electric shock, Le Doux exposed the rats to only the sound of the bell. Despite the fact that these rats had no audio cortex (they could not consciously hear), they exhibited the same stress responses at the sound of the bell that they had exhibited earlier when they had been exposed to both the electric shock and the sound of the bell.

Le Doux proposes a Theory of Indelibility, which states: "Once your emotional system learns something, it seems you never let it go. What therapy does is teach you to control it . . . it teaches your neocortex how to inhibit your amygdala. The propensity to act is suppressed, while your basic emotion around it remains in a subdued form."[2]

However, I, and others, have found that in doing Thought Field Therapy with clients who have been exposed to severe trauma, the nightmares, the intrusive memories, and the exaggerated startle responses that accompany Post Traumatic Stress Syndrome disappear. It would seem that by addressing the trauma directly through the perturbations in the thought field, with its intrinsic relationship with the energy system and nervous system, the emotional charge stored in the autonomic nervous system around a particular trauma-laden memory is permanently dissipated. I believe that the symptoms of post traumatic memories, such as the knee-jerk reactions to events with similar content, the flashbacks, and the intrusive memories can no longer be thought of as permanent. Louie's story illustrates this point.

Using Thought Field Therapy To Treat Post Traumatic Stress Disorder

Louie attended his first session accompanied by his wife, Sue. Three months previous to his visit Louie had been in an automobile accident that had involved a fatality. Since the accident Louie had been drinking too much and was limited in his ability to perform the same tasks at work that he had adeptly performed prior to the accident. Sue was concerned about Louie's mental state, and she was especially concerned about his drinking. Sue felt that she had lost her husband as she had known him. She too was a victim of the tragic accident.

Louie had a second agenda. The accident was not his fault, and he was suing the other driver's insurance company for medical expenses. These expenses would include trips to a Doctor of Chiropractic and office visits with me. In fact, it was Louie's attorney who had initially suggested he see a psychotherapist.

Louie stated that he couldn't get the accident out of his mind. The other driver had made a left-hand turn on a red light and Louie had broadsided the driver's car with his work truck. The elderly woman sitting on the passenger side was killed instantly. The dead woman's husband jumped from the car and yelled at Louie, shouting, "You've killed her!"

Louie vividly remembered the accident as if it were happening in slow motion. He remembered hitting his brakes, sliding into the passenger side of the car, the look on the dead woman's face, and the words shouted by her husband. He remembered the paramedics removing the dead woman from the car. He remembered these things so well that he could think of little else.

Louie was no longer able to drive a company truck as the result of these disturbing memories, so his understanding boss assigned Louie other duties. Still, the only way Louie had found that he could escape these ever-present memories was to drink himself to sleep. Louie agreed with Sue that he couldn't keep on the way he was going. But he didn't know what to do. "I've killed someone and nothing can change that, " Louie lamented.

I tried using some Cognitive Therapy. "I think you're making yourself even more upset by telling yourself you killed this woman. It was an accident. It wasn't even your fault. You didn't plan it. You and this woman were actually both victims of someone else's mistake. You need to keep reminding yourself of these things." But my well-intentioned but somewhat misguided efforts fell on deaf ears.

Before rescheduling our next appointment, I told Louie that we would try something next week that might possibly give him some relief from his suffering.

Louie arrived for his second session accompanied, once again, by Sue. Louie drove as little as possible these days and having Sue by his side during his session was an added comfort to Louie who had never before considered entering a therapist's office.

Louie said that he couldn't imagine how tapping would help, but he was desperate and would "try anything" if I thought it had any chance of helping him. Louie first focused on the incident itself. We used the trauma/anxiety algorithm and when Louie's SUD level had been reduced from a ten to a one, he then reported his SUD level rising back up to a ten. Louie was now focused on the husband of the dead woman saying "you killed her," and he was feeling overwhelmed, this time with guilt. Again Louie reported a SUD level of ten. Tears were rolling down Louie's cheeks as he sobbed, "No matter how you look at it, she's dead, and I did it. I killed her." Again we tapped, this time using the trauma/guilt algorithm. After Louie had reached a SUD level of one this second time, he smiled. "You know" he said, "I'm not feeling guilty anymore. I'm sorry that the woman died, but it really wasn't my fault." "In fact," Louie said, "I'm feeling angry. I'm feeling angry that this man made an illegal left-hand turn and caused this trouble. Look what I've been through."

I asked Louie if he would like to forgive this man for his mistake and go on with his life? Louie replied in the affirmative and we did the Thought Field Therapy anger algorithm. His SUD level was reduced for a third time, this time from a five to a one. Louie commented that he felt like he was "walking on air" as he left the office. I asked Louie to notice during the week what was better and what was not better; in this way we could continue with the work we had begun during this session.

Our next session would be the last time I would see Louie for several months. Louie attended this session alone, and reported that he was feeling relieved of his symptoms of Post Traumatic Stress Disorder. His boss had agreed to let Louie try driving a truck again the following Monday. Louie agreed that he would give me a call and make another appointment if driving the truck, or anything else, triggered any of his old symptoms.

Louie was drinking less, he said, but he needed to keep working on that problem, which apparently predated his trauma. I suggested that Thought Field Therapy could likely help him with this also. But Louie was not a therapy-kind-a-guy and he said that he would try to quit drinking on his own.

I didn't hear from Louie for two or three months. When I did see him again he reported that things were going quite well. He was driving at work and not blaming himself for the accident. Louie stated that he could remember the accident but it was no longer a thought that constantly intruded into his everyday life, leaving him little ability to focus on anything else. He said he still hadn't completely stopped drinking and might want to work on that at a later time. I told him I wasn't going anywhere and would be here if he ever decided he wanted help.

Louie had actually come to ask me to write a letter stating that I had seen him three times for the treatment of Post Traumatic Stress Disorder. He wanted to be reimbursed for his treatment by his insurance company.

This case history above illustrates the limitations of Cognitive Therapy and the benefits of Thought Field Therapy in treating symptoms related to Post Traumatic Stress Disorder. Louie's story also illustrates the "Tooth-Shoe-Lump" effect that often evolves in the treatment of trauma. And we have an excellent demonstration here of the ability of Thought Field Therapy to remove all symptoms of Post Traumatic Stress Disorder quickly and effectively. Additionally we have an example in which Thought Field Therapy was effective despite the fact that the client had little faith in the ability of Thought Field Therapy to be of help.

Louie's Thought Field Therapy Recipes

Trauma/Anxiety
Eyebrow, eye, arm, collarbone
9-Gamut Treatment
Eyebrow, eye, arm, collarbone

Trauma/Guilt
Eyebrow, collarbone, index finger, collarbone
9-Gamut Treatment
Eyebrow, collarbone, index finger, collarbone

Anger
Little finger, collarbone
9-Gamut Treatment
Little finger, collarbone

Treating Trauma When the Abuse Happened at a Pre-Verbal Age

Lottie's mother Doreen was frantic. She had run out of options and had exhausted all therapists in her area who were covered by her insurance plan. She was willing to travel a great distance to try one more therapist. Lottie was nine years old and in danger of being removed from her home because she had been molesting her infant brother. Doreen was beside herself. She loved both of her children. She wanted and needed to protect her son but she did not want to think of her daughter being put in foster care. Time was running out.

Lottie, her mother and her stepfather came to the first appointment and all following appointments together. They related that Lottie did not do well in school and was constantly getting in trouble in the classroom. Her teacher had a system of giving daily stars for good behavior and Lottie had not yet received even one.

Lottie had been sexually abused by her biological father at the age of three and likely before the age of three and he was, at that time, in prison. Lottie couldn't remember the abuse; however she had been told, in a general way, what had happened. Lottie did feel shame about molesting her brother but she didn't seem to be able to stop her compulsive behavior.

I wanted to use TFT to address Lottie's original trauma but decided to begin with a feeling that Lottie was experiencing during the session. Lottie was obviously feeling shame and guilt around the fact that she had been sexually abusing her baby brother and hadn't been able to control her acting-out behavior.

Lottie was a moving target as she flitted around my therapy office, and I decided to use dx rather than algorithms in an effort to keep her attention and hold on to her. I began by having Lottie focus on how bad she felt about what she had been doing. I got a weak muscle and proceeded with the treatment. In no time Lottie's muscle tested strong. I then asked Lottie to focus on what everyone had said had happened to her a long time ago before her father was put in prison. Again her muscle went weak. Again I used dx and soon her muscle tested strong. Not sure what had happened, it was wait-and-see.

When the family returned the next week they reported that Lottie had gotten her first star in school. In fact she had gotten a star every day following her treatment. Her teacher had told her grandmother (who lived with the family), "Whatever you're doing, keep it up." Even more importantly, she was so far behaving appropriately with her infant brother.

Lottie continued to do well in school and her behavior with her brother was no longer an issue. We used the next session to work on her inappropriateness with her stepfather. Lottie's stepfather Howie kept his distance from Lottie because she would try to sit on his lap and compulsively cover him with kisses. I had Lottie stand next to her stepfather and again getting a weak muscle we did the diagnostic treatment until her muscle tested strong. I then had her sit on her stepfather's lap, and repeated the procedure. Finally, I had them lay on the floor near each other and again repeated the process.

We had several follow up appointments spaced farther and farther apart. The good results held up. Lottie got stars at school on a regular basis. And she was consistently appropriate with her infant brother and her stepfather.

Lottie's case illustrates how TFT Causal Diagnosis can help even when the problems originated at a pre-verbal age.

Displaced Anger Due to Early Childhood Sexual Abuse

Nicholas's mother Lydia didn't have insurance and she had little money to spend on therapy. However she wanted help for Nicholas, her youngest son, who was mean to his older brother. For years Nicholas had beat up on and intimidated his brother, despite the fact that his brother was three years older. Lydia had a good theory about why this was happening. Nicholas had been sexually abused by his father to the point that there had been physical damage. The older brother's physical appearance very much resembled the father's. It sounded like a good theory to me and I told Lydia that we could hope to take care of this problem in a few sessions but I could not make any guarantees.

When we met, with Lydia present, I asked Nicholas to focus on his anger at his brother. He had no trouble doing this and we proceeded with the past trauma/anxiety/anger/guilt (just in case) algorithm. Nicholas felt free of anger toward his older brother. I asked him if he felt any anger toward his father for what he had done? He looked surprised and reported no anger. We made arrangements to meet in two weeks, to save Lydia money and to give Nicholas's cure the test of, at least, some time. Shortly before our appointment was to take place Lydia called and cancelled the appointment. Things were normal at home and she would call if needed.

This case study illustrates how TFT can help in a case where the anger is displaced and by curing the displaced anger (the anger at the brother) the anger at the source (anger at the father) is also cured.

Nicholas's Thought Field Therapy Recipes

Trauma/Anxiety/Anger/Guilt

Eyebrow, eye, arm collarbone, little finger, collarbone, index finger, collarbone

9-Gamut Treatment

Eyebrow, eye, arm collarbone, little finger, collarbone, index finger, collarbone

Using TFT Algorithms to Treat Trauma and Depression when the Memories Are Flooding but Keep Changing

It is always best to have the client focus on one discreet memory at a time, especially when you are using only algorithms. In rare cases such as Wilson's this is not possible. Wilson was in his mid-twenties and the sole guardian of his six-year-old son. Two years previous to our meeting he had been viciously attacked at a bar by a complete stranger and seriously disfigured. Wilson almost died, his perpetrator went to prison, and after much surgery, Wilson looked normal even if he didn't feel normal. Wilson felt like he had been ruined and as if his perpetrator had literally stolen his life. Following the attack, Wilson had fallen into a deep depression.

For Wilson, his biggest loss was that, as the result of injuries suffered during the attack, he could no longer taste or smell. Wilson hated to go shopping for food because eating was boring and the grocery store reminded him of his loss. He was experiencing panic attacks each time he would venture into a food market. Wilson worried that his house might be destroyed and he might lose his son in a house fire due to the fact that he wouldn't be able to smell smoke. He had installed smoke alarms but he was hyper-vigilant about unplugging every appliance in the house. Wilson stated that there was no joy in his life and that only the thought of what it would do to his young son kept him from suicide.

Wilson had made several attempts at therapy but nothing had helped. At his attorney's request, Wilson had come to see me, but only to get a professional opinion relative to psychological damage that may have resulted from his victimization.

Wilson did agree, after some coaxing, to try something

new even though he had no faith by now that anything could help him regain his former sense of well-being. In our second session we tried TFT but Wilson didn't feel like it helped. Wilson mentioned that the "Tapping just brought up more memories." I realized that Wilson had not been able to stay focused on just one aspect of his trauma for any length of time.

When Wilson came back for his third session he talked about all the memories our last session had brought up and began to get tearful. I asked him to focus on the memory and accompanying feelings he was now experiencing and began having him tap, choosing spots that would likely be relevant to the feelings he was identifying at the time. After the first algorithm, instead of asking for a SUD (Wilson was still crying) I had Wilson do a reversal correction and while he was tapping the side of his hand, I asked, "And what's going on now?" Wilson said something like, "And now he's standing over me beating my head against the floor." I asked "And what are you feeling as he's standing over your head and beating your head against the floor?" and Wilson said, "Scared, angry, really angry." Again, I had Wilson tap the spots that would likely be involved with these feelings. We did this same procedure for an hour. An algorithm, followed by the question, "And what's going on now?" "And what are you feeling as this is going on now?" The questions were asked while Wilson did the psychological reversal correction and were followed by a new algorithm sequence. Sometimes the memories would be circular and we revisited the same memories from time to time; sometimes these memories would be accompanied by the same feelings; sometimes they would be accompanied by different feelings. At the end of the hour Wilson stated that he felt tired and more relaxed, but no less upset. He described his current SUD level as remaining a ten.

The next week Wilson called to cancel his scheduled appointment saying that he was sick with the flu. Although the flu had been going around in our geographical area, I suspected that he was possibly giving up on this new attempt at therapy. Wilson did call again however, to make a new appointment.

When Wilson walked in, he sat on the couch and said "Thank you. You have given me back my life. I didn't think it was possible. Last week I was sick with the flu and even then, lying in bed, I felt like I had never been happier in my whole life. I'm not feeling depressed. I've made plans to go fishing with my brother. I can shop for food without any feelings of anxiety. And I feel like everyone has to cope with something. I guess I can cope with not being able to taste or smell."

Wilson's case demonstrates that the algorithms can be used even when a client has difficulty staying focused on one aspect of a problem. And his story illustrates that sometimes (very rarely) there is a delayed response to the treatment. I believe that sometimes what looks like a delayed response is actually the client just not making the cognitive shift that change really could have occurred and sometimes it actually is a truly delayed response.

Footnotes

1. Joseph J.E. LeDoux, "Emotional Memory and the Brain," *Scientific American*, 1994, 270, 50-57.

2. Joseph J.E. LeDoux, L. Romanski & A. Xaoraris, "Indelibility of subcortical emotional memories," *Journal of Cognitive Neuroscience,* 1989, 1, 238-243

Chapter 9

Using Thought Field Therapy With Behavioral Therapy

"Treating humans without the concept of energy is treating dead matter."

Szent-Gyorgyi, M.D., Nobel Prize Laureate, Hungary (1893-1986)

❖ ❖ ❖ ❖

For many years, Dr. Roger Callahan, the developer of Thought Field Therapy, specialized in treating anxieties and phobias. In 1980, Dr Callahan began treating these anxieties and phobias with what is now know as Thought Field Therapy. Dr. Callahan soon discovered that these techniques could be used to treat other psychological problems. However, in a typical clinical setting, you will likely be using the Thought Field Therapy anxiety/fear/phobia algorithm more than any other Thought Field

Therapy treatment. The problem you will address almost as frequently will likely be grief.

Using these Thought Field Therapy treatments can often be very straightforward and uncomplicated. In most cases, anxieties or other psychological problems are readily identified, the client has little or no difficulty accessing the emotion and the treatment goes smoothly. I could write about thousands of such cases but I would only be "preaching to the choir." There would be nothing new to be learned, and, if you are reading this book, you already know how effective Thought Field Therapy can be. You are likely more interested in some ideas for using it in more difficult cases.

The following case has been chosen and described in detail, not because it illustrates how easy it can be to use Thought Field Therapy to treat anxieties and phobias and problems involving issues of grief, but because it illustrates how to use Thought Field Therapy and combine it with Behavior Therapy when the problem involves a possible genetic limitation, the answer is not simple or clear-cut, and the treatment is somewhat more complicated and demanding.

Besides using Thought Field Therapy and Behavior Therapy in this case, you will also note the use of an unusual "goggle therapy," and at the very end a very small but perhaps helpful inclusion of Ericksonian Therapy.

Defining the Problem

Darrel appeared confused and awkward when he entered the office. He reported that his marriage was in crisis and he was unsure that he would be able to save his relationship with his wife Joan. Darrel and Joan had been married for thirty-three years and had three grown children. Through the years Joan had become increasingly distressed and upset with Darrel and at this point Joan was apparently unhappy almost all of the time. Both Joan and Darrel were convinced that Joan's unhappiness was due to Darrel's lack of ability to be really present and connected in their relationship.

Joan had told Darrel that she wanted two things from him. She wanted Darrel to be "more in touch with his feelings" and also to be "more supportive" of her. Apparently, even if he accomplished these goals, she was not sure that she could ever love Darrel again. There had been too much hurt, she told Darrel, and she was not sure that she could ever get over the pain of feeling so alone and abandoned in their relationship.

Darrel, a truck driver had always provided a good living for his family and Joan hadn't had to work outside the home, although she stayed busy socially, volunteered at their church, and contributed in other significant ways. Darrel had helped in the home as much as possible, kept the exterior of the home and the yard in order and kept their two cars running. When the children had lived at home, he had spent a significant amount of time with them.

I wondered aloud to Darrel if his wife wasn't, perhaps, a bit difficult to please and he reluctantly agreed that this was true. However, Darrel stated that his wife was unwilling to attend couple therapy. Joan was involved, at that time, in her own individual therapy group. She was tired, she told Darrel, of telling him what she wanted. She had made her needs perfectly clear. Joan wanted Darrel to take care of his own problem. Showing uncommon wisdom, Darrel noted that the only person he could change was himself.

Darrel had come to therapy knowing how he would like to interact in his relationship and in the world. He just seemed to have trouble getting there. After struggling on his own for several years, Darrel was now feeling somewhat hopeless and, at the same time, due to his current situation, he was feeling desperate. Darrel was willing to try anything including therapy.

I asked Darrel to explain to me what he wanted to change about himself. I wanted to help Darrel separate what he wanted to change from what Joan wanted him to change. "If you knew that there was no possibility of saving your relationship, what changes would you want to make for you?" I asked Darrel.

Darrel stated that he really did want to change the things about himself that his wife found so annoying. He, too, felt limited by these behaviors. If therapy were successful he would feel more passion for life and feel more connected to his feelings. He would show more awareness about what was currently going on around him and he would be more connected to and supportive of the person most close to him.

Asking him to be even more specific, he was able to list some specific behaviors that would indicate that he was making progress toward his goals. Darrel stated that he would be showing more personal interest in others, and in particular he would be showing more interest in Joan. He would be remembering to ask Joan how her day went. He would be showing interest in Joan and demonstrating his support of her by remembering to ask her about situations that she was currently concerned and involved with.

He would be showing that he was connecting to Joan and to life by noticing things and commenting on them. He would be saying things like, "I see you're wearing a new sweater. It looks great on you," "Great dinner—I especially liked the broccoli cooked that way; was it lemon sauce?" At home on the patio, he might find himself saying, "I love the way the sun feels. It makes me feel contented and happy."

All this had proved in the past to be a tall order for a nice guy who was relatively introverted and who was, I believe, predominantly left brained. Darrel had grown up in a family where everyone else was also quite introverted, and left brain dominant. The family functioned quite well in its own left brained and introverted way. It was a family of loosely connected individuals who loved and cared for each other. While Darrel couldn't remember any demonstrations of affection or anger, he always knew he was loved and that his parents loved one another. When something was not quite right it was calmly and matter-of-factly discussed. He had no model for and little capacity for being tuned in to others' feelings or his own.

We agreed that it wasn't all that surprising that Darrel would have been attracted to Joan and she to him. In the spirit of opposites attract, they were each initially attracted to a person who acted out, in the Jungian sense, their own shadow side. Darrel was attracted to Joan's ability to be so free and spontaneous in her emotions and so "in touch" with her feelings. This was something he had never learned to do growing up in his family, and something he was possibly not genetically wired to do. Joan, who I later learned was frequently out of control with her feelings, was no doubt initially attracted to the stability of feelings (later interpreted by her as lack of feelings) that Darrel possessed.

Darrel related that he had little ability to even remember to perform the simple behavioral goals that he had previously set for himself. He would get caught up in his daily life and the day would be gone without him having remembered to ask Joan about things that were important to her or to notice anything different about their world. We concluded our first session by agreeing that Darrel would purchase a notepad and that he would keep a list of ideas concerning what he might like to ask Joan about. These questions would pertain to what was going on in Joan's life.

This behavioral intervention proved unsuccessful. When we met for the second time, Darrel hadn't remembered to jot down any ideas. Joan was even unhappier with him, if that could be possible. She accused him of being distant from her and not really knowing her. Darrel felt even more discouraged. He felt that Joan wanted him to be an entirely different person, and Darrel was even more convinced that he couldn't change. I dismissed, for the time being, the idea that Darrel might be forgetting as a way of being passively aggressive. I believed that Darrel's problem was more hard-wired.

After discussing what went wrong with the behavioral intervention (Darrel hadn't remembered to jot down ideas about what to ask Joan about), we came up with the idea of Darrel putting his notepad on the clipboard he kept in his truck. He needed to log his hours on the road and at these intervals he could also stop and think of something that would be of importance to Joan. He would then compose a question or a comment concerning this thing of importance He would pose the questions and/or make the comments in a natural way. With his clipboard as a reminder, this homework assignment had a greater chance of giving Darrel a taste of success.

Introducing Thought Field Therapy

In an effort to introduce Darrel to Thought Field Therapy, and in an effort to create a chance for Darrel to feel some success even during this session, I asked Darrel if there was any anxiety unrelated to this issue that he might want to eliminate from his life.

After thinking for a short time, Darrel confided that he had always had anxiety around money Although Darrel generated an adequate income and his family had never been without, Darrel forever worried that there wouldn't be enough.

Darrel was able to get in touch with this anxiety around money and not having enough and soon his SUD level was reduced from a four to a one by using the simple anxiety algorithm. Darrel felt some success as he left the office. He agreed to notice throughout the following week, whether or not he worried about money and not having enough. He also agreed to put the notepad on his clipboard with his road log. This would serve as a reminder to jot down ideas for questions or comments in an effort to train himself to communicate more intimately with and show more support for Joan.

Addressing a Relationship Dynamic Using Thought Field Therapy

Darrel didn't feel much more encouraged when he arrived for his third appointment. He did report that he had not experienced any anxiety around money or not having enough but qualified this by stating that he hadn't had any reason this week to feel stressed about money. We agreed that Darrel would keep noticing whether things were just the same, somewhat better, or much improved regarding his (former?) anxiety around money and his fear of not having enough.

Despite the possibility that he might have experienced some success relative to his financial anxiety, Darrel remained unhappy. Darrel hadn't sought out therapy to overcome his money fears. Darrel was unhappy because, as he said, tongue-in-cheek, "I want to feel more spontaneous and more extroverted and I want it to happen overnight!" I reminded Darrel that there seemed to be a genetic tendency at play here that might predispose him toward being more introverted and predominantly left brained. I hoped that this information would help Darrel be less hard on himself and I also believed this to be true.

If this had been simply a case about some anxiety getting in the way of Darrel being more connected (which is more often than not the case), the problem would have likely been less difficult to treat. However, I helped Darrel see that with a little work he could develop or activate more connections to his right brain by training and repetition.

In fact, Darrel had managed to do his homework this time and he had posed several questions demonstrating an interest in Joan and he had done this on a daily basis.

Keeping his notepad on his clipboard as a reminder had helped. However, Darrel wasn't sure that Joan had noticed. If she had noticed, she hadn't commented on it. Darrel agreed that he would continue working on this new behavior whether or not it was noticed and reinforced by Joan. After all, this was a behavioral change Darrel wanted to make for himself. He himself wanted to feel more connected to others and more in touch with his own feelings.

Darrel also agreed that he would ask Joan if she had noticed that he had been asking questions about her that were relevant to her life. He would say something like; "I've been feeling more connected to you and hopefully showing more support for you. I've been finding myself asking you more questions that I think are relevant to what's going on in your life. It feels good to me, how is it for you?"

I commented that perhaps, by this time, Joan was only noticing when she didn't get what she wanted and that she wasn't noticing when she did get what she wanted. Or perhaps, I speculated, she was just too afraid to get encouraged by his initial change in behavior. She may not have wanted to get her hopes up and set herself up to be disappointed once again.

I suggested that Darrel might want to ask Joan about some of these possibilities as a way of showing some interest in their mutual relationship and as a way of being more intimately connected.

It sounded like a simple plan but Darrel reported that bringing up such a topic would be much too threatening for him. He volunteered for the first time, as I had earlier suspected, that Joan was not always the easiest person to talk to. And it also became clear that Darrel avoided conflict with Joan at any cost.

Darrel explained that Joan "has a temper," and that he was fearful that Joan would get even angrier with him if he said anything that even hinted that she too might be part of the problem. Earlier on in the relationship, he explained, she might have been happy to have had this conversation. But now there was so much hurt and anger on Joan's part that this seemed too risky. I suggested that what he was doing (avoiding conflict with his wife) wasn't working. Like most people, when what he was doing didn't work, he wanted to do more of it.

Over the years, Darrel had become even more passive and even more non-communicative than he had been previously. He now lived in fear of saying or doing the wrong thing. Joan's anger intimidated him to the extent that he now left almost all decisions up to her. If he made a decision he met with conflict and if he didn't participate he met with conflict. He felt damned if he did and damned if he didn't. So he distanced even more and Joan was presumably experiencing even more hurt as the result of Darrel's distancing.

Darrel needed to do something different. He agreed that what he was doing wasn't working. He had nothing to lose, and perhaps even something to gain, by bringing up subjects that might possibly be a trigger for Joan's anger. At least they would be connected on a more intimate level and Darrel would be showing interest in their relationship.

I asked Darrel if there were something that he would like to talk about with Joan, that he had avoided talking about for fear of triggering her anger. He replied that he would like to ask her to not demean him in front of their friends,something she apparently she did on a frequent basis. This seemed to be a reasonable request and I asked Darrel what got in the way of him addressing this issue with Joan. Darrel replied that he was not comfortable with conflict and, in this case, not comfortable chancing the strong possibility that Joan would be angry with him and reject him. I reminded Darrel that Joan was already rejecting him.

He agreed that it would be in his best interest and in the best interest of their marriage if he made this request of Joan. And he agreed that he would do better in achieving his goals if he were not so intimidated by anger, so fearful of rejection and so avoidant of conflict. Couples who do well are good at balancing their need to be connected with their need to be themselves, and Darrel was losing himself in an effort to stay connected and it wasn't working. Darrel agreed to do some tapping before the close of our session in an effort to reduce his anxiety around conflict.

As Darrel focused on the thought of asking Joan to refrain from berating him in front of their friends, he obtained a SUD level of "four or five" (a high level of feeling for Darrel). When we finished the anxiety algorithm Darrel reported "just a trace" of nervousness. He agreed to bring up this one problem with Joan before our next session. I also gave him a copy of the anxiety algorithm to take with him. In this way he could treat his anxiety around bringing up something negative with Joan if any of the anxious feelings returned or if new ones came up. And, of course, Darrel would continue using his clipboard to remind him to jot down ideas that would help convey caring and support to Joan.

A Turning Point

The fourth session marked a turning point in Darrel's therapy. He reported that he was able to approach Joan with his request that she not speak negatively about him in front of their friends. Joan's initial response, as Darrel had predicted, was one of anger. Despite Joan's initial reaction, Darrel was somewhat surprised to notice that he was experiencing only a very slight level of anxiousness both in bringing up the problem and in the resulting aftermath. Later, Joan apologized for her angry outburst but continued to maintain that she "only told the truth" in front of their friends. However, Joan's behavior did in fact change and Darrel reported that Joan was no longer exposing his shortcomings to acquaintances. This change reportedly lasted over the period of time that I met with Darrel.

Darrel had learned that he could survive an episode of Joan's anger and upset. He was no longer intimidated by her anger and, he was remembering to verbally show more concern and support for Joan. Despite these changes, Joan's attitude toward Darrel did not change and Darrel was unfortunately not feeling any more connected to his feelings. He wanted to experience more of the "highs and lows" of life. Instead, he felt emotionally flat.

In our initial interview I had determined that this lack of feeling was likely not due to depression or Dysthimia. And this problem didn't seem to be connected to any anxiety that either Darrel or I could get a handle on. Darrel very much wanted intimacy and did not seem to have any fears around closeness. Addressing his fear of conflict, while a constructive step toward intimacy, did not address Darrel's lack of ability to feel.

As we spoke about Darrel's lack of feeling I had the idea to perform a little experiment with the idea that we might possibly find some evidence to substantiate our hypothesis that Darrel was in fact working predominantly from his left brain. We did some "goggle therapy." I instructed Darrel to put on a special pair of goggles that I had constructed from inexpensive plastic safety goggles. These goggles had duct tape covering all but the extreme right edge of the goggles.[1] When Darrel looked through these safety glasses, he was, in fact, isolating his left-brain. Looking through the goggles, Darrel attempted to picture or feel, but there were no pictures and there were no feelings.

I then had Darrel slip on a second pair of goggles, similarly constructed, with the exception being that these safety glasses had duct tape covering all but their extreme left edge of the goggles. Wearing this pair of goggles, Darrel was experiencing the world primarily through his right brain. Darrel was quite surprised with this demonstration. While wearing this pair of spectacles, he could picture quite vividly and he could experience some feeling. Darrel felt more hopeful that he could strengthen the connections in his right brain.

While this "goggle therapy" is not a treatment in and by itself, I frequently make use of these goggles to illustrate a point. When people are "of two minds" about some issue in their life, they often feel quite different about the issue as they isolate their right brain as compared to when they isolate their left brain. After experiencing this in reality rather than the abstract clients are usually more hopeful about their ability to solve a dilemma. They understand why they "think" one way and "feel" another way. At times I have treated a problem (with TFT) with the goggles on as a way for the client to be emotionally in touch with a problem as we tap.

As Darrel's time would be limited with me, due to insurance restrictions, I offered some suggestions and ideas for Darrel to experiment with in an effort to help Darrel in his efforts to be more in touch with his feelings via developing more connections between his right and left brain. These suggestions included doing Steven Rochlitz's[2] brain integration exercise, possibly doing some sound therapy such as Somonas Sound Therapy [3] which is available on CD's, and continuing his efforts to be more in touch with others and himself.

Some Progress

At the beginning of his fifth session, Darrel reported feeling like he had made progress. With the help of his notepad reminders, he was remembering to express an interest in what was going on in Joan's life. He was occasionally bringing up a topic that he knew would likely trigger Joan's anger but a topic that he felt they needed to talk about. And he was no longer experiencing anxiety around money.

However, he still felt unconnected to his feelings, with the exception of some feelings of grief and anxiety. The grief and anxiety Darrel felt, stemmed from the fact that there had been no change in Joan's attitude toward him. She was still angry with him and reportedly expressed her anger on a regular basis. Darrel was unsure that she would ever get over her anger, and he felt the ever-present threat that she might end the relationship.

Darrel and I agreed that the grief and anxiety he was feeling at the time was not helpful to him in his efforts to change. His sadness and fear were likely getting in the way of his efforts to feel more connected to his more positive feelings. We agreed to use Thought Field Therapy a third time.

Darrel focused on the anxiety and grief he was feeling around the status of his relationship with Joan. Darrel loved his wife and desperately wanted to save his marriage. But Darrel wasn't sure that he would be able to make enough changes to please Joan. He wasn't sure if there was anything he could do at this point that would enable Joan to love him once again. The feelings of sadness and anxiety around the possibility that his wife might never again feel love for him and might subsequently divorce him were feelings that Darrel had very little difficulty getting in touch with.

Using the combined grief/anxiety algorithm, Darrel's sadness and anxiety around his precarious position were successfully reduced. When Darrel left the office after this fifth visit he was still very much focused and concerned about his status with Joan; however he was not stuck in the disabling feelings of grief and anxiety that he had originally come in with. Darrel would, hopefully, be freed to work on the positive changes he needed and wanted to make in his life.

Darrel would continue in his efforts to talk with Joan about difficult and not difficult things. He would continue using his notepad to help him in his efforts to be more aware of what was going on in Joan's life and to be appropriately supportive. And we added one new homework assignment.

During the session Darrel had commented on how unaware he was of his surroundings. Perhaps if he could become more aware he could begin to experience some feelings, for instance joy over the beauty around him, such as the wildflowers he passed on the roadside as he drove his rig. Or perhaps he could find amusement watching the birds playing in his backyard. I suggested that Darrel purchase a small talisman to keep in a place on his person, like in his pocket, where he would likely encounter it on a regular basis. When he touched the talisman, it would be a reminder to stop, capture the moment and attempt to get in touch with the pleasure of the experience of now. No thinking about the past, no thinking about the future, only experiencing the now.

A Summary of Progress

Our sixth and last session consisted of summarizing our progress and summarizing our accumulated ideas for exercises that might help Darrel feel more connected.

We both agreed that Darrel was doing much better at showing support for Joan and in connecting with her. Darrel still needed the help of his notepad to remind him about these things, but I expressed hope that this would eventually become more spontaneous. In an Ericksonian kind of way I said something like, "And as time goes by you might find that you are doing these things naturally and spontaneously without the help of your notepad, or maybe you'll find yourself using the notepad occasionally to remind you to continue to do the good work that you have started here in these sessions…"

We agreed that, since Joan was not interested in doing couple therapy, he could only concentrate on working on the part of the problem that was his. Thanks to Thought

Field Therapy, Darrel was no longer afraid to bring up issues that had a potential for triggering Joan's anger. This new dynamic held potential for developing a more intimate relationship. And, thanks to Thought Field Therapy, Darrel was no longer experiencing anxiety around money. Finally, Thought Field Therapy had helped Darrel control his grief and his fear around the possibility that Joan might not want to stay married to him.

As Darrel had just purchased his talisman (a small pocketknife) and was just beginning to use it to remind himself to be more aware of his surroundings, I did a second brief Ericksonian intervention that I had prepared in my mind ahead of time and said something like:

"And as you use your talisman to become more and more connected to your surroundings you might find yourself at the same time being more and more connected to life. I don't know if being more and more connected to life will help you get more connected to your feelings in a very short time or whether it will take a longer time, but either way you will perhaps find yourself being surprised that you are being less hard on yourself knowing that you are doing so many good things to help yourself to develop a feeling of being more connected to your surroundings."

Darrel had not yet worked the Rochlitz Brain Integration exercise into his schedule and I suggested he find a way to do this in an effort to perhaps establish more connection to his right brain. I encouraged him to buy the Rochlitz book that contains this exercise and explained that Rochlitz had discovered that the effectiveness of the exercise was likely due more to the fact that it involved the supraspinadas muscle (this is the muscle that, in oriental medicine, is connected to the brain meridian) than to the fact that in doing this exercise the arms cross the midline.

He might also think about listening to some of the music I had previously mentioned that is specially engineered to activate the right brain (such as some of the CDs produced by Somonas Sound Therapy).

I have included this case study in detail not because it has a fairytale ending and not because it illustrates how Thought Field Therapy can quickly and dramatically change a client's life. Neither of these things happened. Rather, I have included this case study as a demonstration of how Thought Field Therapy can be combined with a variety of behavioral techniques when time is limited and you are treating a problem that likely involves genetics and hardwiring.

Darrel's Thought Field Therapy Recipes

Anxiety
Eye, arm, collarbone
9-Gamut Treatment
Eye, arm, collarbone

Grief/Anxiety
Eyebrow, eye, arm, collarbone
9-Gamut Treatment
Eyebrow, eye, arm, collarbone

Our last case study involves a young girl who was not well liked at school. Her behavior was immature and she did not seem to have developed an age appropriate sense of right and wrong. In the four sessions described below, there were significant behavioral interventions but after a startling revelation by the mother of this girl, it was TFT that dramatically saved the day.

Helping a Young Girl By Treating Her Mom

Tammy was concerned about her eight-year old daughter Sabrina. Sabrina had been described as mean and cruel by her teacher, and was not well liked by her peers.

Sabrina's teacher had requested that Tammy have Sabrina tested for ADD. However, in our first session, I ruled out ADD as an explanation for Sabrina's poor behavior. Tammy reported that Sabrina read voraciously, did her homework without prompting and accompanied her parents on long road trips without becoming bored. Sabrina received excellent grades in her academic studies. However, she did not handle frustration well. Her mother reported that Sabrina threw tantrums when she didn't get her own way, both at home and at school.

Rather than being ADD, I suspected that Sabrina, an only child, was overindulged and suffering from the "too precious child." syndrome. I stressed to Tammy how important it was that Sabrina learn to tolerate frustration. I emphasized that learning to tolerate frustration in an age-appropriate way is a skill critical to becoming a mature adult capable of healthy relationships.

Not allowing a child to develop and mature in this area is handicapping a child and, although usually well intended, is a form of child abuse. It is often the parent who is handling their own anxiety by preventing the child from facing frustration and learning to develop age-appropriate coping skills. I usually frame this problem to the parent in a positive way, using a re-frame technique I learned at a class sponsored by The Mental Research Institute in Palo Alto, California. I tell the over-indulgent and/or over-protective parent that they are being "too good a parent."

I talked to Tammy about setting some simple rules and consequences that she and her husband would agree to enforce consistently. I emphasized that the consequences had to be well thought out, enforceable and effective. Tammy agreed to give rules and consequences a try.

Seven months later, Tammy returned with Sabrina (who I sent to the waiting room) reporting that the rules and consequences had been successful at home, *i.e.* Sabrina was no longer throwing temper tantrums at home when she didn't get her own way, but at school, rules and consequences even though enforced weren't getting to the basic problem. Sabrina's teacher reported that her behavior at school remained disturbingly cruel; hitting, shoving, and saying mean things. Needless to say, Sabrina's behavior had not made her any friends among her classmates.

Among other things Tammy and I explored the possibility that Sabrina had not developed a conscience. I suggested that she begin reading stories with morals and talk about moral dilemmas as a way to get Sabrina to begin developing appropriate empathy and responsibility for her actions. Tammy's assignment was to read or tell Sabrina stories that presented moral quandaries. Sabrina would be asked to discuss what she thought a particular character should do and why? When situations arose naturally, Tammy might use these opportunities to have a spontaneous discussion with Sabrina. The homework was not to teach Sabrina some didactic concept of "right" and "wrong" but to stimulate moral thinking and to kindle the development of empathy and responsibility.

During the period of time that Sabrina was invited into the therapy room with her mother, (about 20 minutes) I noted that she continually made "cute" faces, looked at her mother (apparently to see if she was looking at her) and, overall, displayed babyish behavior.

I suggested to Tammy that she leave Sabrina at home the next time she visited the office. We needed to talk.

It was the third session and Tammy sat on the couch unaccompanied. She reported that Sabrina's behavior was already improving. Tammy had even received a "Thank you" after purchasing a small item for Sabrina, an act that Sabrina formerly would have been taken by for granted. Both Tammy and her husband had been taken aback by this unexpected and un-typical behavior. Sabrina had also expressed some sadness around an injured animal whose story had been reported on the news. We both agreed that the stories, their moral dilemmas and the reflections and discussions had likely been beneficial.

In this same session I called Tammy's attention to my previous observation that Sabrina's behavior was immature for an eight-year old child. I proposed that this "cutesy behavior was likely highly annoying to her classmates. Tammy agreed that other children are frequently annoyed with Sabrina, and that Sabrina has learned to be annoying to get attention. With uncommon courage Tammy admitted that she had in fact babied Sabrina because it made her sad to think of her only child growing up and leaving home.

Tammy began to cry at the very thought of her child growing up. We used Thought Field Therapy to address this sadness and soon Tammy was expressing disbelief at feeling so comfortable with the thought of an empty nest.

Tammy came to our fourth and what would be our last session stating that she was encouraging Sabrina to act her age. “Perhaps”, she wisely said, “Sabrina has been taking care of me by not growing up.” “Now,” she stated, “I am giving Sabrina the freedom to act her age.”

Seeing Tammy turned out to be more important for Sabrina’s mental health, than seeing Sabrina would have been. Tammy cancelled a fifth session that had been scheduled saying that already there had been dramatic and noticeable changes in Sabrina’s behavior both at home and at school.

The above scenario illustrates what most of us already know: A child’s problem is seldom about the child. Treating Tammy made it easier for both Tammy and Sabrina to begin the process of healthy individuation. With Tammy no longer dependent on Sabrina, Sabrina was free to differentiate and move toward more age appropriate behaviors and to eventually become a differentiated adult capable of maintaining healthy relationships.

Footnotes

1. Fredric Schiffer, M.D. (1998) New York: The Free Press *Of Two Minds: The Revolutionary Science of Dual-Brain Psychology*

2. Steven Rochlitz, Steven. (2000) Sedona, AZ *Allergies and Candida with the physicist’s rapid solution*

3. Sononas Sound Therapy www.somonas.com

Chapter 10

FAQ
(Frequently Asked Questions)

Recognizing that some readers may want to re-familiarize themselves with some of the material that was presented during their Thought Field Therapy Training, I have included this chapter and presented it in question and answer form for the reader's convenience.

Why is Thought Field Therapy called Thought Field Therapy?

For many years Thought Field Therapy was simply known as the Callahan Techniques. In fact Dr. Roger Callahan frequently refers to Thought Field Therapy as CTTFT or Callahan Techniques Thought Field Therapy to distinguish his constantly updated, refined and validated discovery from its many offshoots that also claim the name Thought Field Therapy.

In science, a field refers to an invisible area of influence. For example, Einstein has shown us how gravity bends space and time and yet no one has ever actually seen gravity. We see only the effect of gravity. Large objects in space maintain a predictable relationship to one another and large objects stay steadfast on the surface of the earth rather than flying off into outer space. We attribute these effects to the gravitational field.

Similarly, we cannot see a magnetic field, but we do not question its existence when we see metal objects attracted to an electrically charged magnet.

During my Thought Field Therapy Algorithm Trainings I ask participants to perform a simple experiment. I ask them to, for a very short time, focus on something from the past that was sad or traumatic for them. I remind them that if they focused on this for a long enough time, they might begin to feel different. They might look in the mirror and even notice that they look different. Friends might see them and say, "What's wrong? You look troubled." This demonstrates the influence of a particular thought field. On the other hand, I could ask them to think about something that they were really looking forward to, or a pleasurable experience from the past. Again, they might find themselves feeling very different. They might look into the mirror and notice that they looked different. Friends might say, "You look like you're feeling on top of the world." Once more, we witness the influence of a specific thought field.

You cannot do Thought Field Therapy without tuning into a thought field. The client will need to focus on the specific problem that is to be worked on. If we were trained acupuncturists and were doing acupuncture for a physical problem, the patient would not be asked to think about anything in particular. As a trained acupuncturist, we would be working on a problem pertaining to the body. However, we are concerned here with issues of thoughts and their corresponding emotions. The thoughts must be present in order to work on them. The more you use Thought Field Therapy, the more I believe you will appreciate why it eventually came to be known by the name by which it is now known. When Thought Field Therapy is successful the feelings and emotions previously paired with a specific thought field have been permanently changed.

What do I do if my client can't get in touch with the feelings around a specific thought or situation while in the office?

You can still do Thought Field Therapy even if the feelings around a specific thought are not accessible to the client while in your office. The client may say something like "I want to work on my road rage but I can only get upset when I am driving and somebody does something stupid." If you are trained in Thought Field Therapy at the diagnostic level you have an advantage, as muscle testing will often detect the distress, even when the client is consciously unaware of it at the time. However, if your training is limited to the algorithm level you can, in many cases, get good results. You need to begin in the usual way, by having the client tune in to or think about the problem. In the case of road rage, the client would be thinking about a typical situation, which might trigger the emotion in real life, like a slow driver or someone pulling out in front of him.

Then, have the client do the:

Recurring PR (rubbing the Neurolymphatic Reflex Point)

Major Treatment

9-Gamut Treatment

Repeat of Major Treatment

Mini-Reversal (again rubbing the Neurolymphatic Reflex Point)

Major Treatment

9-Gamut Treatment

Major Treatment

Floor to Ceiling Eye Roll

(The recurring reversal spot was used because it frequently works when the psychological reversal correction spot doesn't. However this is the only kind of a scenario where you would want to begin by using this particular correction.)

You have now treated your client's presenting problem using an algorithm that may or may not have been effective. Your client has however, had some practice using these techniques. You may want to tell your client that although what you have done together may have been helpful, only time and exposure to the specific problem treated will tell. You will give him the instructions for doing this himself and he will need to practice the technique so if the problem arises he can treat himself if needed. You will want to warn the client not to wait until the situation arises to practice this technique. It may be too difficult (especially in our hypothetical case, which involves road rage). It is important to have a supply of handouts with easy to use directions for using the algorithms to give to clients when they leave a session such as the one described above.

In a much different kind of scenario a client may report that they can't get in touch with a difficult feeling they know is present somewhere "underneath." They may report feeling numb when they think about this feeling. Have them rate their numbness on a scale of one to ten. Address the feeling of numbness using the appropriate major treatment spots. Usually this would include the complex trauma algorithm points with possibly the anger point and/or the guilt points or any other points that you surmise might be involved. Often this lowers the feelings of numbness and the feelings begin to surface. When this happens you can again pick the appropriate algorithms to deal with the underlying emotions.

How do we distinguish between fear and anxiety?

Fear usually refers to an excitatory sympathetic nervous system response that is experienced about something imminent or in the present. According to the *American Heritage Dictionary*, fear is: "1.a. A feeling of agitation and anxiety caused by the presence or imminence of danger. b. A state or condition marked by this feeling. 2. A feeling of disquiet or apprehension."

Anxiety is also an excitatory sympathetic nervous system response. However, anxiety in general refers to worry or anticipatory fear about something that might happen in the very near or more distant future. The *American Heritage Dictionary* describes anxiety as: "1.a. A state of uneasiness and apprehension, as about future uncertainties.

b. A cause of anxiety. 2. Psychiatry. A state of intense apprehension, uncertainty, and fear resulting from the anticipation of a threatening event or situation, often to a degree that the normal physical and psychological functioning of the affected individual is disrupted."

A phobia is an irrational fear about a specific thing. According to the *American Heritage Dictionary,* a phobia is "1. A persistent, abnormal, or irrational fear of a specific thing or situation that compels one to avoid the feared stimulus. 2. A strong fear, dislike, or aversion."

The distinction is not really all that important because whether you are dealing with anxiety, fear or phobia, if you are using a Thought Field Therapy algorithm, it will be the same algorithm.

Can letting go of fear be dangerous to a client?

I suppose it could, but I have yet to encounter a situation where helping a client let go of a fear or an anxiety presented a danger. Keep in mind that we can be concerned and/or cautious about a situation without being anxious or fearful. It is understandable that fear has a protective function in the case of infants and small children. It undoubtedly plays a role in protecting animals who posses little or no ability to reason. But fear and anxiety more often than not interfere with our ability to be safe as adults.

I think that most people would agree, for example, that a person who is driving a car at the same time they are experiencing an anxiety is a less safe rather than a more safe driver. And a woman who is in an abusive relationship and is fearful for her life may be enabled to gather the skills to leave the relationship once she gets rid of the immobilizing fear that has kept her trapped and kept her unable to focus on implementing a plan of escape. She can be cautious and concerned about her situation without being paralyzed by the anxiety trapped in her nervous system.

What about grief? Don't clients need to grieve significant losses?

Of course they do. They just don't need to be stuck in their grief forever. In the earlier stages of grief, clients often report being stuck with an unwanted memory, such as the memory of a person's contorted and unnatural face as they were dying. Clients sometimes report being able to think of little else but such a disturbing image. Treating such a client with the grief algorithm can allow the client who has just experienced a significant loss to remember the good times and the happier days they have experienced with that loved one. There is still sadness, but much less trauma. Letting go of stored trauma helps the client feel more connected with the departed one and facilitates the grief process.

At other times, clients come to us because they feel like they have been stuck in their grief for too long a time. (Too long a time is what the client defines as too long a time.) Using the grief algorithm can help these clients move on. In working with grief it's usually helpful to define the goal as "peace and acceptance." In other words, a SUD of one would mean a feeling of peace and acceptance rather than an "absence of grief," which might sound unacceptable to the client.

Sometimes clients need their anger, don't they?

Anger can sometimes be helpful. For instance, anger often indicates a significant turning point in therapy when a client begins to get angry with a perpetrator rather than feeling angry at themselves or feeling guilty or depressed. Anger can be the initial motivator of change. But anger held onto, whether held inside or acted out, becomes harmful to the person stuck in the anger and, at times, can also be harmful to others.

Research abounds demonstrating the connection between anger and resentment on one hand and cardiovascular disease on the other. A great deal of research also contradicts the once-popular notion that emoting is a good way of letting go of anger. Rather than healing anger that has been "held in," research demonstrates that emoting, in many cases, only makes it worse.[1] We can remind clients that they can be righteously indignant about something (for instance child labor in third world countries) without being, in an emotional sense, angry. We often need to remind clients that the anger is hurting them and they need to let go for their own sake and not necessarily for the sake of the other with whom they are angry.

One last thought about anger is that we sometimes need to help clients understand that letting go of anger and even offering forgiveness does not automatically necessitate contact in any way with the person against whom you no longer harbor anger and/or resentment. My favorite definition of forgiveness is a quote from Robert Enright: "Forgiveness is letting go of resentment to which you are entitled and offering to that person friendlier feelings, to which they are not entitled."[2] Helping clients think about their anger in these kinds of ways often facilitates their willingness to work on resolving their anger.

How do I decide whether to use the guilt algorithm or the shame algorithm?

Guilt is usually about something that was done, or not done. Shame is usually a feeling about oneself. Listen to the language your client uses.

An additional thought about guilt: There is a somewhat popular notion that guilt is a bad thing. While it can be unhealthy, the ability to feel guilt is a positive thing. People who do not have the capacity to experience guilt are, at the minimum, sociopaths, and at the extreme, psychopaths. If no one ever felt guilty this would not be a desirable state of affairs.

However, clients often feel inappropriate guilt, or hold onto guilt much too long. When working with inappropriate, or formerly appropriate guilt that has been held onto, it is good form to ask the client to "to tune into the feelings of guilt," as opposed to "tuning into the guilt."

My clients frequently report that they feel frustrated. What algorithm can I use to treat frustration?

A client may present with a problem or situation and they may describe their feelings as ones of frustration. "When things don't go perfectly, I get easily frustrated."

I think of frustration as a feeling of low-intensity anxiety. Often, the feeling of frustration is low-intensity anxiety combined with low-intensity anger.

These feelings can be addressed successfully in most cases with either the Thought Field Therapy anxiety algorithm or the combined Thought Field Therapy anxiety/anger algorithm. After successful treatment clients who feel frustrated when they are not in control, for instance, will feel no feelings of frustration or anxiety around the fact that their ability to control has its limitations and they are, ultimately, not in complete control.

When working with depression, on what do you have the person focus?

This is usually not so much a problem due to the fact that depressed people are already in this state. They can't not tune into the problem. Paying attention to the words a client uses to describe their depression can be helpful. You might suggest that they tune into their feeling of hopelessness or that feeling of lack of excitement about life. I once worked with a young man who was not attending school due to his depressed state. He denied being depressed but stated that he was "bored."

In this young man's case we tuned into his feeling of boredom and his SUD level of "boredom" was reduced from a ten to a one by using the depression algorithm.

How about working with pain when there is more than one area of pain?

As a general rule, focus on the most intense area of pain first and when that has been reduced, focus on the next most intense area and so on. Pain that moves around is encouraging. Energy is moving and something is happening. In some cases the pain's "movement" from one spot to another may actually be the result of the "Tooth-Shoe-Lump" effect.

When working with addictions, what can I do to insure that my client uses this method to reduce addictive urges when not in my office?

Unlike most other Thought Field Therapy treatments, the addictive urge treatment will need to be repeated by your client whenever their addictive urges begin to build. They will need to do this treatment for a period of time. This time can be very short for some clients and much longer for others. Nothing you can do will gurantee that your clients will comply. Doing the homework, any homework, is often an issue when it comes to addictions. Whether the prescribed treatment is taking a medication that reduces the cravings, taking a medication that has an aversive affect, AA attendance, or using the TFT addictive urge algorithm, ultimately clients controls their own success. However, proper preparation can greatly increase your client's chances of compliance and therefore success.

Whenever possible, ask your client to come in for their session actually experiencing the addictive urge. If they are a smoker, for instance, and their goal is to quit smoking, it is ideal for them to come in wanting a cigarette. They should not smoke a cigarette immediately before entering your office. You can then provide an opportunity for your client to experience the difference that using the addictive urge/anxiety algorithm can make in reducing their craving.

Explaining to the client that they have been suffering from anxiety and have been medicating it with an addictive substance or an addictive behavior can be an immense relief to the client, who is usually suffering at the time from a great deal of shame around their addiction. Shame itself fuels the addictive cycle. Shame leads to anxiety (about self) and ultimately to the addictive behavior that at least temporarily medicates the intense feelings of anxiety. Using the technique of congratulating the client for having found a way to medicate his or her own anxiety, in my experience, can be paradoxically helpful. This then leads to a discussion and a resulting agreement that there are problems associated with the way they are currently self-medicating. This is a good time to introduce the TFT addictive urge algorithm as a way to eventually eliminate the anxiety and as a direct result, a way to eliminate the addictive urge. They can then try the anxiety algorithm in your office and experience how it works for them.

In my experience this simple algorithm is almost always successful in that moment and brings the addictive urge down to a one. The client now has a new tool, a new way to self-treat their anxiety. This new way of treating their anxiety is a way that will not cause additional problems in their life, is inexpensive, has no negative side-effects and is easy to use. Eventually, they will need to tap less and less as their various anxieties are reduced.

It is helpful, when the client is a one, to have them (in the case of smoking) get their cigarettes. Have the client look at them, hold them, and take a dry drag. Do any of these activities raise the SUD level even slightly? If the answer is "yes," again do the addictive urge/anxiety algorithm until the client is a one.

Have the client visualize various situations in which they might engage in their addictive behavior. In the case of smoking, this might be the first cup of coffee in the morning, taking a break during working hours with colleagues who also smoke, or before retiring for the night. If any of these visualized situations bring up any urge, once again, use the addictive urge algorithm until the situation no longer brings up the urge to smoke.

Send the client home with instructions for doing the algorithm. Ask the client to practice this treatment when she is not experiencing the urge to smoke. When she does begin to feel the urge, ask her to treat herself early, before the urge is at a ten. If the urge is already at a ten, the chances are much less that she will actually use the algorithm.

Some offshoots of Thought Field Therapy always begin by rubbing the recurring psychological reversal correction spot? Wouldn't that often save time?

Only a few clients need to rub this neurolymphatic spot, located on the left side of the body. Many don't need a reversal correction of any kind, and for the majority of those who do need a reversal correction, the simple psychological reversal correction (tapping the side of the hand on the little finger side) is sufficient. If you automatically correct by rubbing the recurring psychological reversal spot with every client, it not only wastes time for the majority of clients, but you are missing out on some very important information about those clients who do need this treatment. If a client responds to a treatment only after rubbing the recurring psychological reversal spot, this strongly suggests that toxins are involved. This is a critical piece of information for both the therapist and client. The client may already know what substance they are ingesting or breathing that is toxic for them and this can be a reminder. Or, alternatively, you may want to refer to a physician or other professional, such as a therapist trained in TFT at the Dx level or the VT level, who is trained in identifying Individual Energy Toxins (IETs).

When tapping a specific energy point, does it make a difference which side of the body is tapped on?

No. You can switch from one side of the body to the other during the same treatment.

I have seen people tap on both sides of the body. Is this even more powerful?

There are 12 energy meridians and they are mirrored on either side of the body. In the beginning, when Roger Callahan first discovered what eventually became know as Thought Field Therapy, he had clients tap simultaneously on both sides of the body. Through the years he discovered that tapping on both sides of the body is unnecessary. Tapping on only one side of the body is equally as powerful as tapping on both sides.

Two treatment spots used in Thought Field Therapy are located on the midline of the body so tapping on one side or the other is not an issue with these points. These two points, one located under the nose and the other under the lower lip, utilize points on the two major connecting vessels that connect the meridians in the front and back of the body. The connecting vessel that runs up the front of the body is the central vessel and it is tapped in the algorithm for the treatment of shame. The governing vessel runs down the back of the body and it is tapped in the treatment of embarrassment, Level II reversal, and nasal congestion.

What about alternative tapping spots when one or more of the standard Thought Field Therapy treatment spots can't be used?

There are rare occasions when the usual tapping spots cannot be used. A nurse who had taken my training called one morning to tell me that a patient she wanted to treat with Thought Field Therapy couldn't be tapped on the beginning of her eyebrow or under her eye because she had been brutally beaten. I was able to remind her that the beginning of the eyebrow is one end point on the bladder meridian. The other end point is located on the outside, bottom corner of the little toenail. The corresponding end point for tapping under the eye would be the other end of the stomach meridian which would be located on the second toe (the one next to the big toe) on the bottom corner of the nail on the side facing the little toe. She was able to successfully treat her patient for trauma and anxiety using little toe, second toe, under the arm, collarbone.

At times clients, especially those being treated for depression or pain begin to feel physical irritation when tapping the gamut point. The alternative endpoint for the gamut spot would be the outside end of the eyebrow. The 9-Gamut Treatment could be done using this spot as well.

A therapist attending one of my algorithm trainings reported that she had been an avid scuba diver until recently when after putting on her mask and gear and dropping under the water she became overwhelmed with fear. Her last dive ended with a serious panic attack. At the time of the workshop, just the sight of her mask would set her into a panic. Her husband was also a diving enthusiast and she wanted to join him again in their underwater fun. Because she couldn't get in touch with her fear of diving without her mask as a trigger, she asked if she could bring her mask to the second day of the training.

During the second day of the training she put on her mask, and reported that on a scale of one to ten, her SUD level was around a "twenty". Because the mask was on her face, I decided that this would be a perfect opportunity to try tapping on the other end of the stomach meridian (the toe spot) instead of on the usual spot under the eye. We used "toe/eye/collarbone" as the major treatment or tapping sequence to treat her intense anxiety around scuba diving. The woman soon reported a SUD level of one but in challenging this (with her mask still on) she reported that she had just a little feeling left in her stomach. As I was preparing to address this she said "No! Wait a minute. Its just excitement that I feel." She shared that she had been picturing herself underwater with fish swimming around her. "I can hardly wait to get down there and swim with the fish." The intervention seemed a "toe-tale" success!

For a description of the alternative tapping spots refer to the TFT Treatment Spot Locations—Appendix II.

When I first learned to do Thought Field Therapy, there was an affirmation that was taught that accompanied doing the various psychological reversal corrections. Why isn't that taught in approved Thought Field Therapy trainings anymore?

Thought Field Therapy is a therapy technique in process. It is constantly being refined in an effort to add only what actually enhances the effectiveness of the treatment and eliminate anything that does not enhance the effectiveness of the treatment. When Dr. Roger Callahan discovered how to correct psychological reversal in 1979, he realized that psychological reversal frequently had to do with a person not accepting himself or herself just as they were at the time. He appreciated that accepting ourselves as we are is, paradoxically, the first step toward eliminating a problem.

So, for a long time tapping on the side of the hand or rubbing the neurolymphatic reflex point was accompanied by the words "I deeply and completely accept myself, even though I have this problem." This was said three times while continuing to tap or rub depending on which spot was being used. While correcting for a mini-psychological reversal, the words repeated were "I deeply and completely accept myself even though I still have some of this problem." For the deep level psychological reversal, the words were "I deeply and completely accept myself, even if I never get over this problem." said three times while tapping under the nose. After some experimenting several years ago, Dr. Callahan discovered that the affirmations were unnecessary. Beyond that, they were frequently confusing. Some therapists erroneously got the idea that these were times to install positive affirmations. Thought Field Therapy does not involve using positive affirmations.

Eliminating these affirmations was very difficult for me at first. Like most people, I can be resistant to change. However, I found that Dr. Callahan is correct. The affirmations apparently added nothing. I achieve the same great results without using these affirmations.

If I am not reversed and I tap or, in the case of the recurring psychological reversal spot, rub a reversal spot, can it reverse me?

No. When in doubt, correct the reversal. You cannot cause a psychological reversal by tapping on the psychological reversal correction point or by rubbing the recurring psychological reversal spot.

Why is it suggested that I tap along with my client?

Thought Field Therapy is best learned by doing. If you model the technique, explanations can be kept to an absolute minimum and the client can simply mirror what you do as you verbally direct them to "tap under their eye right on the edge of the bony ridge," etc. This way you won't have to present the client with a course on how to do Thought Field Therapy.

A second and equally important reason for tapping along with your client is that clients tend to feel a little silly at first, doing this unorthodox treatment. If you are tapping along with them it will tend to reduce their self-consciousness around performing these unusual activities.

Can I tap too much?

Besides taking the chance of bruising yourself by tapping too hard, or too long, there is no harm in tapping, nor does the technique lose its effect over time.

What does all this tapping do to the therapist?

It doesn't appear to do anything. When you are tapping along with a client you are not, of course, tuned in to your own problems. However, if you are empathetically tuned into your client's problem, I suspect that this might enhance the effectiveness of the client's treatment. I base this suspicion on the interconnectedness of all things including human beings as proposed by quantum field theory.

How do I handle the "Tooth-Shoe-Lump" dilemma when it arises?

"Tooth-Shoe-Lump" refers to the phenomena of a new problem arising after successfully treating the original presenting problem. There is a tendency for more intense pain to mask less intense pain. Sometimes this new problem is unrelated to the original problem and sometimes it is another layer of the original problem.

> Although, "Tooth-Shoe-Lump" is usually about more intense pain masking lesser pain, sometimes the opposite is true. Sometimes clients even create minor physical pain to take their mind off of a pain that is psychological as in the cases of clients who cut or otherwise mutilate themselves. The physical pain provides them a welcome distraction from their psychological suffering. Other clients may create a psychological crisis in their life or sometimes a compulsive series of dramas to alleviate a deeper psychological pain that they are avoiding. A client in intense physical pain may welcome the presence of a novel pain. I once had a client who had suffered with chronic rheumatoid arthritis for most of his life who told me "This probably

> sounds crazy, but sometimes it feels good when I hurt myself because it takes my mind off the pain that is always with me."

The unusual and colorful name "Tooth-Shoe-Lump" is derived from an actual event in Dr. Roger Callahan's life. Suffering from a severe toothache, Dr. Callahan was able to get an emergency appointment with his dentist. While sitting in the waiting room, his dentist came out and gave him an injection to ease the pain. When the pain subsided he realized he was wearing an ill-fitting pair of shoes that hurt his feet. After removing the offending shoes, he then noticed that the waiting room couch that he was sitting on was lumpy and uncomfortable. Thus, "Tooth-Shoe-Lump."

Using Thought Field Therapy often enables a client to feel different about a situation in a very short period of time. More often than not, however, there are other problems to work on or there are other as yet un-addressed aspects of the same presenting problem. This can be where knowledge of the "Tooth-Shoe-Lump" effect is helpful.

If a client's SUD level goes down to a one and then says, "I have another issue I'd like to work on," you would of course, simply just proceed to the next problem. But sometimes it isn't that straight-forward.

A client may say, "I'm back to a ten" (or some other number higher than one) and as you inquire about the problem you find that the client is now tuned into a different aspect of the same issue you have been working with. There might be a different feeling involved. For example, the client may have been focusing on anger and now is experiencing the sadness that was beneath their anger.

This will be treated as a new problem; you are treating a different feeling related to this original problem. This is a simple example of "Tooth-Shoe-Lump."

There will be times when a SUD level is lower, but not a one, and a new feeling related to the original problem arises. This is a more complicated version of "Tooth-Shoe-Lump." If the client can separate the feelings, continue working on the original feeling, and come back to the newly uncovered emotion later, in a separate treatment. If these feelings can no longer be held separately in the client's thought field, and you are using algorithms, begin again, using a proper combination of points to address the entire spectrum of emotions now involved related to this problem. You will now be starting at the beginning of a new treatment, this time with a new, likely more complex algorithm.

What are some other reasons that SUD levels may not be going down?

Assuming that you have gone through the process of correcting for psychological reversal, recurring psychological reversal,and Collarbone Breathing, you might ask yourself if you have defined the problem clearly and concisely. If not, you may be attempting to work on too many issues at once and/or the clients is tuned into, and is skipping around through several different thought fields at once. Especially when training is limited to the algorithm level, it is important to do a thorough job during phase one, the phase of clearly defining the problem.

It could be a "Tooth-Shoe-Lump" problem and the client is no longer focused on the same exact problem. Remember, in rare cases, just tapping on one or two spots can reduce the original problem to a one. You need to make sure the client is still focused on exactly the same problem. For more about this refer to the question pertaining to "Tooth-Shoe-Lump" above.

There may be allergies or energy sensitivities involved. If the client is wearing fragrance, this could be interfering with the treatment. Ask the client to attend the next scheduled session fragrance free. No scented laundry detergent, fabric softeners, hair sprays, lotions, and of course, it goes without saying, no perfumes, colognes or essential oils.

The client might need a more complicated treatment and may need to be referred to a diagnostically trained therapist or, if you are a diagnostically trained therapist and are already using TFTdx to treat the problem, the client may need to be treated by a therapist who is equipped to do Thought Field Therapy Voice Technology.

Remember, no therapy works all the time for every one, but in most cases you will find that, if you do a good job setting up the problem (phase one), even the simple algorithms developed by Dr. Roger Callahan will work. Those trained at the diagnostic level know how helpful this next level of training can be in helping the therapist obtain even higher levels of success using Thought Field Therapy. Voice Technology has the greatest success rate of all forms of Thought Field Therapy and is usually reserved for the most difficult to treat cases.

How about when the SUD level has gone down, but then becomes stuck at a lower SUD level?

If you have already done a mini-psychological reversal correction and repeated the entire algorithm that you began with and the SUD level is not a two or below, there may be a feeling connected with the original problem that you were not aware of and perhaps even the client was not aware of. You probably need to talk some more with the client, especially if you are limited to using algorithms. The missing feeling may reveal itself by simply talking to the client. You might have missed the fact that the client was also feeling guilt (or anger, or sadness, or anxiety, or shame, or embarrassment) relative to the problem that you have been working on. You can start again with a new algorithm combination that includes the guilt algorithm (or other appropriate algorithms). If upon checking, all that remains is a feeling of guilt (or other feeling not originally identified) simply have your client do the appropriate algorithm. For a further discussion of this kind of difficulty see the question pertaining to "Tooth-Shoe-Lump" in this chapter.

Footnotes

1. B. J. Bushman, R. F. Baumeister, A.D. Stack, "Catharsis, aggression, and persuasive influence: self-fulfilling or self-defeating prophecies?" *Journal of Personality and Social Psychology*. 1999, 76. 367-376.

2. Michael J. Farrell (1997)" They say you can do yourself a favor forgiving others," *National Catholic Reporter, 1997, pp 9-11.* Also: William A. Meninger, "The Process of Forgiveness" in Muller-Fahrenholz, *The Art of Forgiveness.* WCC Publications

APPENDIX I

Thought Field Therapy Glossary of Terms

Thought Field—A field of influence paired with a particular thought. Tuning in to the thought field (thinking about the problem that is to be dealt with) is necessary in order to treat a psychological problem using Thought Field Therapy.

Algorithm—A sequential treatment pattern including a Major Treatment the 9-Gamut Treatment and a repeat of the Major Treatment. Algorithms are patterns that were discovered by Dr. Callahan to be successful a great majority of the time for specific psychological problems.

Major Treatment—A part of the TFT treatment process involving a sequence of tapping on specific meridian points in a particular order, used at the beginning and the end of an algorithm or in TFT dx, or VT the beginning and end of a holon.

Nine-Gamut Treatment—An entire range (the "whole gamut") of activities that are performed while continually tapping on the Gamut Spot (located on the back of the hand just below and between the knuckles of the little finger and the ring finger).

Perturbation—A disturbance in the normal energy pattern. Negative emotions are proposed by Dr. Callahan to be caused by perturbations in the thought field.

Psychological Reversal—A disturbance in the energy system, which prevents, until it is eliminated, the problem from being dealt with effectively.

- Recurring Psychological Reversal—A psychological reversal that is repetitive, usually due to toxins.
- Mini Psychological Reversal—A psychological reversal that occurs later in the treatment, after an algorithm (or holon) has been completed with partial success.

SUD Level—A subjective measurement standing for Subjective Units of Distress.

Appendix II

TFT Algorithm Treatment Spot Locations

The **Arm Spot** is located on either side of the ribs about four to five inches directly under the arm.

The **Eye Spot** is located directly under the center of either eye on the bony ridge. There is a tiny notch in the bone at the exact point, but if you use two fingers, you don't have to be exact. (WARNING! If you or a client has long fingernails, use the knuckles to tap.) An alternate spot would be located on the second toe (the one next to the big toe) on the little toe side, near the lower corner of the toenail.

The **Collarbone Spot** is located about an inch down and two inches to either side of the sternal notch in the depression below the clavicle.

The **Eyebrow Spot** is located at the beginning of either eyebrow by the bridge of the nose. (Watch that clients don't tap too high on the forehead.) An alternative spot is located on the outside of either little toe by the lower outer corner of the toenail.

The **Little Finger Spot** is located on the thumb side of either little finger near the lower corner of the nail.

The **Index Finger Spot** is located on the thumb side of either index finger near the lower corner of the nail.

The **Gamut Spot** is located on the back of either hand in the depression below the base joints of the little finger and the ring finger. An alternative spot is located at the outside end of the eyebrow.

The **Psychological Reversal Correction Spot** is located on the little finger side of the outside of either hand midway between the base of the little finger and the top of the wrist bones.

The **Recurring Psychological Reversal Correction Spot** is found by going one inch down from the sternal notch and going about four or five inches over to the left. This is not an acupressure spot, but a neuro lymphatic reflex point. (Note: The neuro lymphatic reflexes were discovered by Frank Chapman, D.O. in the 1930s.) This area is rubbed in a circular motion rather than tapped. When this intervention is needed this spot is frequently quite tender or even painful to rub.

APPENDIX III

Corresponding Acupuncture/ Acupressure Points

This reference is included for those who are interested in locating the treatment points as they are located on an acupuncture or acupressure chart.

TFT Treatment Spots	Meridian Location	Energy Point
Eye	Stomach	ST 1
Eyebrow	Bladder	BL 2
Arm	Spleen/Pancreas	SP 21
Outer Eye	Gallbladder	GB 1
Collarbone	Kidney	K 27
Little Finger	Heart	HT 9
Middle Finger	Pericardium or Circulation/Sex	CS 9
Index Finger	Large Intestine	LI 1
Gamut Spot	Triple Burner or Triple Warmer or Thyroid	TH 3
Psychological Reversal Correction	Small Intestine	SI 3

TFT Treatment Spots	**Meridian Location**	**Energy Point**
Recurring Psychological Reversal Correction	Neurolymphatic Reflex Point *(Not a Meridian)*	
Nose	Governing Vessel	GV 26
Lip	Central Vessel	CV 24
Thumb	Lung *(Used Only at Diagnostic or VT Level)*	L 1
Liver	Liver *(Used Only at Diagnostic or VT Level)*	LIV 14

APPENDIX IV

A Brief Summary of Research Using TFT

Thought Field Therapy has been used successfully in the treatment of a great majority of difficult psychological problems. Most research has been in the area of first hand clinical observation and the personal reports coming from therapists and clients have been impressive. One formal investigation, conducted in early 1995 by Charles R. Figley, Ph.D. and Joyce Carbonell, Ph.D. of the Psychological Stress Research Program and Clinical Laboratory at Florida State University yielded impressive results in the treatment of Post Traumatic Stress Disorder.[1] For this study, four new treatment approaches were selected on the basis of previous merit. These methods were: Traumatic Incident Reduction (TIR); Visual Kinesthetic Dissociation (NLP); Eye Movement Desensitization and Reprocessing (EMDR); and Thought Field Therapy (TFT). Figley reports that:

TFT stood out from all other approaches of which I am aware because of five reasons:

1. It is extraordinarily powerful, in that clients receive nearly immediate relief from their suffering and treatment appears to be permanent.

2. It can be taught to nearly anyone so that clients can not only treat themselves, but treat others affected.
3. It appears to do no harm.
4. It does not require the client to talk about their troubles, something that often causes more emotional pain and discourages many from seeking treatment.
5. It is extremely efficient (fast and long lasting).[2]

Another impressive study was done by Dr. Joyce Carbonell.[3] Her study specifically targeted acrophobia, a fear of heights. Subjects who met the cut on the Cohen Acrophobia Questionnaire (Cohen, 1973) were randomly divided into two groups. They were also asked to give a subjective report of their discomfort (SUD) while climbing a ladder.

The Carbonell study was double blind as neither the therapists nor the subjects knew which treatment they were receiving. One group was treated with the Thought Field Therapy trauma/anxiety algorithm, and the other group received a placebo treatment that included the psychological reversal treatment and the 9-Gamut treatment (both legitimate components of TFT). After treatment, subjects were again given the Cohen Acrophobia Questionnaire and again asked to give a subjective report of their discomfort (SUD) while on a ladder. When comparing pre-treatment and post-treatment scores on the Cohen Acrophobia Questionnaire and pre—and post—SUD scores, the Thought Field Therapy group was significantly more improved by subjective report (SUD) and by objective report (The Cohen Acrophobia Questionnaire) when compared to the placebo group.

A previous investigation using Voice Technology (VT), an advanced TFT technique developed by Dr. Roger Callahan in 1985, yielded similarly impressive results[4]. Voice Technology is a more technical and advanced form of TFT which requires special equipment and is even more effective than Thought Field Therapy at the diagnostic level. Especially difficult clients are treated by phone or even on the radio using this advanced form of Thought Field Therapy. In a 1986 study, 68 subjects were treated for distress and/or anxiety over the radio by Dr. Callahan in an average treatment duration time of 4.34 minutes. 97 percent of these subjects were successfully treated in this short time, with an average improvement of 75.9 percent. Glenn Leonoff, Ph.D. of Monterey, California, replicated this study ten years later in 1996. Also using Voice Technology, Dr. Leonoff treated 68 subjects over the radio in an average treatment time of 6:04 minutes. The average improvement in this group was 75.2 percent.

In the year 2000, a group representing The Global Institute of Thought Field Therapy traveled to Kosovo. 105 subjects were treated for extreme Post Traumatic Stress Disorder. 249 traumas were treated, 247 of them successfully. Kosovo's equivalent of our Surgeon General has made Thought Field Therapy the official trauma treatment of Kosovo[5]. Thought Field Therapy has also been demonstrated to elevate Heart Rate Variability (a higher heart rate variability or HRV is positively correlated to overall physical well being) in clients suffering from anxiety, chronic pain, fatigue, stress, trauma, grief, phobias, and depression.[6]

My own personal clinical experience using Thought Field Therapy has been that over 95 percent of my clients are, in a very short time, by their own report, cured of one or more of their presenting problems after the use of in-session Thought Field Therapy.

Footnotes

1. M. Wylie, "Going For The Cure" *Family Therapy Networker*, 1996, July/August pp. 21—37.

2. Glen R, Schiraldi, Ph.D. (2000) Los Angeles, Lowell House, *The Post Traumatic Stress Source Book. p. 23*

3. J. Carbonell, J. "An Experimental Study of TFT and Acrophobia". *The Thought Field*, Vol. 2. Issue

4. G. Leonoff, G. "Successful Treatment of Phobias and Anxiety by Telephone and Radio," *The Thought Field.*

5. Carl Johnson, M. Shala, X. Sejdijaj, R. Odell, K. Dabishevci, "Thought Field Therapy-Soothing the Bad Moments in Kosovo," *Journal of Clinical Psychology*, 2001—57 (10), 1237-1240

6. R. Callahan, "The Impact of Thought Field Therapy on Heart Rate Variability," *Journal of Clinical Psychology, 2001-* 57, 1153-1170

INDEX